BUYING AND MAINTAINING PERSONAL COMPUTERS

A How-To-Do-It Manual for Librarians

Norman Howden

HOW-TO-DO-IT MANUALS FOR LIBRARIANS

NUMBER 98

NEAL-SCHUMAN PUBLISHERS, INC.
New York, London

Published by Neal-Schuman Publishers, Inc.
100 Varick Street
New York, NY 10013

The paper used in this publication meets the minimum requirements of American National Standard for Information Sciences—Permanence of Paper for Printed Library Materials, ANSI Z39.48–1992.

Printed and bound in the United States of America.

ISBN 1–55570–376–3

Library of Congress Cataloging-in-Publication Data

Howden, Norman.
    Buying and maintaining personal computers : a how-to-do-it manual for librarians : Norman Howden.
        p.   cm. — (How-to-do-it manuals for librarians ; no. 98)
    Includes bibliographical references and index
    ISBN 1-5557-376-3 (alk. paper)
    1. Libraries—United States—Data processing.   2. Microcomputers—United States.
  I. Title.   II. How-to-do-it manuals for libraries ; no. 98.

Z678.93.M53 H69 2000
004.16'024'092—dc 21   00-027652

CONTENTS

PREFACE

People might look at you a little strangely if you claimed today that microcomputers were a means of freeing the masses from enslavement to computer specialists, but that's exactly the way we thought about them in the 1980s. Big "mainframe" general-purpose computers became available in the 1960s. Two decades later, after suffering endless project delays, after dealing with computer bureaucrats, and facing enormous costs to engineer new applications, computer users were pretty fed up. Those two decades ended with an abrupt turn into the tumultuous microcomputer revolution in 1980.

Libraries bought into the revolution in many ways. Plenty of libraries walked slowly into technology, still conscious of the cost and constrained by a low level of staff readiness and parent organization funding. Many libraries out there today may just now be adding their first computer. The most adventurous or visionary librarians jumped in wholeheartedly, whether through directly purchasing early model computers or products that had a microcomputer at their heart. Whether fast or slow, the steady change had produced tremendous results. The overall result has been the proliferation of access to databases, enormous changes in self-sufficiency, and the first steps into the world of the library without walls.

Buying and Maintaining Personal Computers: A How-To-Do-It Manual for Librarians examines the momentous role computers continue to play in the life of the modern library. Microcomputers provide subject access, circulation control, and entrée to resources outside the library. Patrons may have remote (i.e., home) access to the library catalog as well as the library's database resources, the Internet, and community information. Microcomputers are plentiful, increasingly inexpensive, and becoming incredibly useful for entertainment as well as work. While not crucial in every library, in many reading rooms it would be impossible to provide the scope of access to users without the use of computers and telecommunications. Advanced telecommunications and full-text document delivery seem to be the immediate future for most libraries. Computerized indexes, particularly, reduce search time from hours—with paper indexes—to minutes.

As computer networking leads us to a new era of centralization, microcomputing has made desktop computers ubiquitous. Desktop computer users need to improve their productivity through access to other computers as well as organizational databases. Organizations have responded to the productivity needs, but quickly moved to a phase of minimizing the personnel resources and number of servers invested in local area networking. The chance that some balance may be struck emerges. Everyone sees the value of centralizing networks, so long as access to individual computing is not impaired. Eager to harmonize users and support agencies, professionals involved with supplying computers for their organizations know there are many areas that require work.

We have all watched the expansion of new technology in libraries. Devising ways to put new technology in place has always entailed changing something in the library organization or the nature of library work. My responsibility in writing *Buying and Maintaining Personal Computers: A How-To-Do-It Manual for Librarians* has been to introduce library science students and managers to the considerations that need to be made in what is essentially a process of organizational growth. Judging new systems, collaborating with colleagues on key decisions, and planning for the future collectively created an ongoing process of technological examination. Staff must learn new tools and skills while procedures and policies must adapt to a new environment.

The ideas and recommendations presented will help you achieve the maximum in long-term value.

For librarians there is a definite need to find the place to start; one showing an overview of "how the game is played." Many resources exist that provide great detail about technology, networking, computer repair, and specific software packages. Here you will find methods to move beginners forward with technology—particularly those managing small libraries and information centers. In the process, you will discover new ways of making decisions and the best way to integrate choices with your library operations.

Buying and Maintaining Personal Computers: A How-To-Do-It Manual for Librarians researches many specific areas to develop a sharp knowledge base about managing technology. Seasoned librarians will find useful tips to enhance their best practice repertoire. Newcomers to technology will gain the time necessary to develop intuition while saving the valuable time expended by the "hard knocks" experience of their predecessors.

Exploring technology management raises many formidable questions to librarians. Key chapters answer crucial questions:

What is life cycle costing and why is it important?

Do new technologies require policy and operational changes?

What hardware should be purchased?

What software might be needed?

How will technology be supported in the library?

Along with the explanations in the text are a number of forms for record keeping and problem solving. The book includes extensive appendixes offering ready-made documents to place my recommendations into practice. These forms are not final versions of materials and will no doubt need a local touch to be completely useful. A Website at *www.smu.edu/~nhowden/micros.html* contains word-processor copies of those forms. Please download them and modify them as needed. The forms are freely given for non-commercial use but are not to be copied for use in other publications without permission.

One of the primary hopes that come with this book is that library managers will more fully understand and participate in efforts to implement life cycle costing. Many organizations, particularly in the field of education, continue to be confined to unwise budgeting procedures that are rooted in a fixed cycle without long-term plans for capitalizing needed technology. It is the responsibility of managers to advance beyond the mesmerizing aspect of technology to also insure that resources are fully and wisely used.

Flexibility and innovation with technology encourages professionals to think imaginatively. Managers will experience these creative aspects themselves, assuring and affirming the process in others. Developing oneself and nurturing growth in fellow workers is one of the most wonderful outcomes of implementing new technology. This knowledge promises to enhance the advancement of your entire library.

1 PLANNING

The first step in deciding how to acquire and support microcomputers is to look at computing from the viewpoint of users in the organization. Imagine the notions that typical librarians might have if they've spent enough of their spare time wandering through the local appliance marts and computer stores. They probably have some idea that they can purchase computers to do a lot of the publicity work, pathfinders, and schedules for library activities with a good desktop publishing program, some clip art libraries, a database program to manage mailing lists, and access to a good laser printer. The library director may already use a spreadsheet to simply keep track of the budget. It could be that the director has already thought for some time now that it would be a good idea to share all that information with the staff. Good feedback could help cure the problems caused when somebody overspends the portion of the budget devoted to a subject area within collection development.

From the perspective of the library professionals I've just described, it would seem that the computer systems are a free-flowing resource that has begun to bear expectations, however reasonable, rather similar to Aladdin's genie. This is a not an uncommon syndrome that users have because it is easy to detach the expectations for computing from the real-world arena of resource availability. Users often have no idea what arrangements the larger organization makes for implementing computing and how it is possible to affect that agenda. Even more likely is that the library will benefit from a chance budget surplus, buy new technology, and not have the means to maintain or upgrade it. Will we get new computers when the ones we have now are obsolete? Can we buy a new printer to keep up with the other departments that have moved into fast laser printers and away from dot-matrix and ink-jet printers altogether? Will we upgrade to the new version of our word processor? Can we find the funds to gain access to the Internet? Each of these questions can probably be answered in a reasonable way, if the organization is willing to get involved in life-cycle costing and the process of planning computing resources to meet operational needs.

The key issue for today's library manager is the way the computer's life cycle and cost cycle are managed. Only a few years ago we were all very affected by the simple question of whether we had a computer that would empower us. Today we find that not just possession, but quality of operation is terribly dependent on whether our computers are going to be upgraded, maintained, and replaced. With current technology we can communicate, author, teach, and create in the best ways possible. The only way those things will happen is when the library is able to build microcomputer costs into parent organization philosophy and budgets in such a way that they become the normal process of business. That objective is achievable if the life cycle costs are defined and planned for in a realistic way.

LIFE CYCLE COSTING

Life cycle costing and insertion of that cost into organizational procedures and practices can be a challenging task. This process requires understanding the organization, costing the life cycle, then tailoring cost to make the best organizational integration possible (Oberlin, 1994). The steps involved in making life cycle costing work begin with gathering and assessing information about the organization:

- Analyze budget procedures. Each organization has a process and local forms that are followed in preparing budgets. To work within the process it is important to know how to insert and justify new items and to modify current items. It's useful to know the people who govern the budget processes, the start/end date for the budget, and organizational goals that are superimposed on the budget.
- Obtain definitions for cost categories within the budget. Within the budget it is necessary to know the categories for computer equipment, software, and computer and printer supplies.
- Know the historical budget for the library in technology related areas. In addition to the overall budget increases and declines, how have technology funds varied in recent years?
- Know if there are specially budgeted funds or funds from external sources. Academic organizations, particularly, often have grant money or state and local funds that are used to fund certain categories of computer equipment. Occasionally a local organization, such as an employee group, student group, or special interest group, will fund technology just as they might fund a book acquisition. In school libraries and public libraries funding may need to be integrated into bond packages.

Cost-out the technology required for library operations:

- Prepare an estimate of cost for library computers and software. It is important to be aware of unique computing requirements that may be uncovered in the estimation process so that they can feed into the budget justification. Electronic reserves, for instance, may require high speed printers for output.
- Estimate the useable life of hardware and software. Equipment

may have a useable life for its intended use but do not count its extended life if it is retired to some other purpose.

INTEGRATE THE COSTS WITH THE LIBRARY BUDGET AND MISSION OBJECTIVES

Fit the annual costs to the best locations in the budget. Life cycle costs must fit into budget categories that best match, but there may be room for ingenuity usually due to the parent organization making it easier to justify certain categories. It may be possible, for instance, to purchase repair support as either a contract service, a consultant service, or an internal transfer to another part of the organization.

Estimate costs that will not fit the budget or the budget categories. Items that exceed the organization's budget ceiling may have to be funded from some other source.

Find creative financial resources to cover any difference between estimated life cycle cost and the amount budgeted. Some obvious sources include: charge back to patrons, acquisition as part of library materials budget (use this one carefully), external grants, internal grants, friends of the library and other donations, and transfer from library revenue (copy service profits or patron fines).

Examine tradeoffs and adjustments to determine where equipment and software configurations can be changed to less expensive options or fewer pieces of equipment. Adjustments should not impair library performance. Decrease of performance in one area may be compensated by improvements in another.

A checklist to use as you begin assessing the organization is included in Appendix A. A worksheet for equipment and software items is included in the Life Cycle Costing checklist found in Appendix B.

STRUCTURING THE TECHNOLOGY BUDGET

Beyond the process of learning about the organization and finding creative solutions to funding are the basic realities of organizational economics. Many technologists feel that libraries, along with other organizations, take a sometimes unrealistic view of implementing technology (Kinnaman, 1995). To implement as large a cost as technology can be may require restructuring the budget completely and may require adjusting time-honored priorities.

Before you can reasonably manage an organization's computer resources, it is important to know something about the organization. Almost every library has a parent organization and one or more groups of users, euphemistically called "publics," that may affect how library operations are appreciated, funded, and carried out. Library technology must be linked to the funding process of the organization, just as the public service program is. Ideally, this means knowing that the costs associated with particular computers are essential to having certain programs, information products, or services available in the library.

In order to outline a strong program of technology management for the library, this book will examine the following topics:

- Life cycle costing
- Developing computer resources
- Choosing applications software
- Choosing hardware
- Choosing utilities
- Configuration management
- Setting up shop
- Support
- Software policy
- Tools and supplies

The balance of this first chapter will be devoted to the problem of planning and identification of goals—both in the short term for continuity as staff changes and strategically as the organization changes. Continuity planning is an important aspect of the problem of organizational assessment that can confront either a totally new library or one that is experiencing a turnover in staff. Strategic planning spins the web of communication that allows the library to meet the needs and expectations of the parent agency with the minimum of friction and dislocation.

DEVELOPING A TECHNOLOGY PLAN

Individual staff members in the library have unique conceptions of how technology will be used, as do individuals in the parent organization and among library users. The process of developing a technology plan provides the opportunity to reach a consensus on a common concept and to commit the necessary resources for life cycle support of the chosen technology. Technology plans are rather different than some other operational plans, however, because they must contain within them a commitment to reexamination of the environment and future technology in such a way as to permit substantial change rather than institutionalization of a particular technology. Such a change might, for instance, result in a decision to change over to workstation technology that operates under a new and different operating system or an annual commitment to determine which vendor to use for annual purchases. Invariably, the plan must also permit alignment with new methods of teaching and instructional deployment.

The process for developing a technology plan should be very similar to strategic planning and other forms of long-range planning. The steps in the process will probably include the following:

- Choose objectives for the technology plan that realistically portray what outcomes are desired. This might include such things as providing access to the online catalog, access to the Internet, access to databases, developing desktop publishing, adding electronic books, or improved financial management. For educational organizations, objectives should support specific educational programs or support improvement of teaching outcomes.
- Outline the most likely technologies that will allow the library to achieve the objectives.
- Analyze the timing in relation to other library programs that will affect when and how the technology is implemented. This, for instance, may mean that new technology is installed after completion of a building program or that it will be installed after the parent institution completes installation of an Ethernet local area network (LAN).
- Define the impact that the chosen technology will have on library users, staff productivity, and—if possible—the organization's effectiveness or bottom line.
- Define the support required to maintain the technology: how quickly repairs must be effected, what percent of equipment must be working at any given time, which computers have priority for upgrade and repair.
- Assess the need for upgrade and replacement during the period covered by the plan.
- Estimate the total cost of expendables, ergonomic materials, and training assets during the period covered by the plan.
- Define the life cycle of the plan and the replacement rate for each type of technology the library uses. Computers, data projectors, servers, and telecommunications equipment all need to be replaced at some point.

Technology plans are sometimes carried out primarily as cost allocation programs, but to realistically put life cycle costing to work requires more. In many ways the technology plan is the heart of life cycle costing because it documents the details that are needed to fully implement the process.

CONTINUITY PLANNING

When you first walk into a new organization, there are a lot of questions you might ask, but the one I always enjoy asking is where the printer manuals are kept. Printers have a tendency to get set up, then run reliably for long periods of time. By the time a first maintenance problem surfaces, the manual for the machine has probably migrated across several desktops and will take days to find. In an organization where people care, the manual is located in an easy to find location with other manuals or in proximity to the machine it covers. The concepts that I have in mind when I'm locating the manual include:

- Technology belongs to the entire library staff, not just to the most knowledgeable user or technician
- Systematic control of computer parts, manuals, and supplies is economical and the best way to provide initial troubleshooting assistance when something goes wrong
- Personnel turnover doesn't have to result in major turmoil
- When equipment is retired, transferred, or in surplus, documentation can go with it for whoever ends up as the owner
- The degree to which library staff respect resources may be reflected in the way they are able to care for them

From one year to the next a lot of change goes on in libraries. Physical building space may not increase, but the resources in the building will almost certainly change. Ranganathan was right when he pointed out that "a library is a growing organism." The collection will be developed and weeded, new electronic resources will become available, and patrons' demands will change. Only if we plan for change to affect the way we do business will we cope effectively.

The first rule of thumb I would offer is to do it now. Assess technology resources and implement configuration control before your organization goes another day. Every time I've walked into a situation where I've had a predecessor, it's taken a month to know where all the manuals and other resources are and longer to know the status of all the equipment, software, and processes. Configuration control is discussed in a later chapter, but controlling resources we can tackle right away.

Most libraries and information centers need to take some immediate steps to be sure they know where key resources are located and to be certain that they will continue to be there. Key steps include:

- Locate manuals for the currently owned computers and make sure they are located where they will be accessible: a pamphlet box in the vicinity of each computer or a set of shelves in a central location.
- Be sure supplies are stored in a secure clean environment. Computer components and supplies are affected by temperature extremes and dust, so closed cabinets in an office environment are required.
- Establish a central location for unused components that will keep them from getting lost. Spare cables, remote controls, extra printer trays, and other optional parts often are left laying near computers. These parts get lost in the ground clutter and in public areas are tempting for pilferage.
- Establish a protocol of labeling parts detached from machines. In the process of troubleshooting it is easy to lose track of which component came from which machine and what equipment it is compatible with.
- Set up a procedure for tagging broken equipment whether the part is broken, repairable, or new. A staff member needs to routinely move parts to repair sites, to salvage, or to technicians for installation. If the status of parts can't be identified there is a real danger of wasting labor and parts resources.
- Know the location, identity, and configuration of all the microcomputers in the library. Simply numbering or naming the machines systematically will save the time of technical staff responding to maintenance and upgrade requests.
- Insure microcomputers are not vulnerable to theft, including security engraving. Engrave the library inventory number on the case, and take other security precautions. In public areas, adequate security may require security cables on every machine. In some areas you may need security cameras that feed to video recorders.

There are some very important steps that can be taken to reduce the confusion when staff turnover occurs. The first is to be sure that files are properly maintained. Files that document purchasing decisions—even if they're old tattered spiral binders—can be very helpful in tracking what decisions were made and why. Then there is a need to know where the following resources are located:

- Tools for computer maintenance—technicians should sign receipts for their toolkits when first employed.
- Original copies of software—original disks should be housed in a central file.
- Software site licenses—an inventory that establishes the scope of licensing should be maintained in paper or computer format and in a safe location. (Backed up if in computer format.)
- Software individual licenses—paper licenses that come with software should be filed along with the license numbers that activate the software. Since activation numbers often are affixed to manuals, they may need to be transcribed.
- Hardware—inventory listings should identify each computer and its major components as unique items.
- Surveys—original security, wiring, and configuration surveys used in planning facilities should be on file. When facility expansion or revision is needed it's good to have a starting point.
- Plans and proposals for spending and program development— often such sources document assumptions about the environment and provide an outline to guide spending over several budget years.
- Maintenance plans and histories—help technicians plan and track the work they do.
- Network schematics and port assignments—are essential to troubleshooting network problems and for adding new service. IP addresses, in particular, are used frequently as new database services are added.
- Backup systems and data—insure that a computer that has been damaged in some way can be restored to operation in minutes rather than hours.
- Data archived from projects—which may be publicity materials, public area program materials, plans, grant proposals, and other important materials that require extensive compilation should have safe storage locations.
- Technology proposals and budgets—need to be both safely stored and publicly accessible. Staff buy-in is a lot easier if everyone is included in the planning process and can see that funds are wisely spent.

With these resources identified, the next task should be to insure that all of them are checklisted for accountability anytime there is a personnel turnover. This could be accomplished quite simply by insuring the materials are filed in a file cabinet that all staff have access to. An overall procedure should be developed to designate which person in the information center is responsible for which resource. As personnel enter and leave the organization, custody of key resources should be transferred in an orderly and accountable manner.

IN SUMMARY

To whatever degree resources are professionally controlled, most libraries will wish to assess and manage microcomputers as efficiently as possible. The high dollar cost for the equipment and software, added to the cost for training personnel, suggests that microcomputers are a resource that demands serious management thought and action.

2 LIFE CYCLE COSTING

Every book its reader
Every reader his book
Save the time of the reader
Save the time of the staff
The library is a growing organism
                              —Ranganathan

Like Ranganathan's observation that libraries grow, it should be something of a corollary that technology usually represents a process of change. As a forceful element of change in the organization, it stands to reason that we treat technology dynamically in the management process. In financial terms, that means considering the whole life cycle as something that is planned for rather than as a traditional equipment or media purchase.

Much of our decision making about purchases and support for technology needs to be conditioned by the communal experience that libraries have had with technology. One factor seems to stand out in that communal experience: technology has moved from being a support system into a new role as one of the primary conveyances of information. In many ways we can no longer do our work without the assistance of computerized databases, communication networks, and software systems. Looking at computing technologies particularly, the change has meant that libraries are challenged to have up-to-date computers, good communications, and resources that can be accessed through computers. How do we insure that the new reliance on technology can be kept viable within the library?

Life cycle costing is one key element to keeping technology fresh and workable in the library. It is not the sole element. The library has to be committed to doing its mission in the best way possible. Resources must be available to support technology. Talent to set up and keep the technology working is essential.

WHAT IT IS

Life cycle costing is simply a way of responding to the need for repair, upgrade, and eventual replacement. Buzzwords are often used to describe this approach, including "total cost of ownership" and "fully maintained cost."

Ideally, life cycle costing should be part of an effort to design or manage for cost. As defined by Ed Dean at NASA (Dean, 1996), the process of designing for cost is centered on meeting cost goals by reengineering a product or process while maintaining high quality standards. Defined this way, design for cost is an orderly method for finding new alternatives for accomplishing a goal and considering the alternatives based upon cost. In library terms, designing for cost involves changing the options for technology in a way that will still deliver the quality information service the user needs while finding the most cost effective means of doing so.

The most direct method of insuring that computer systems will meet quality, cost, and user goals is to: 1) understand the total cost of acquiring computer systems, 2) include training and support costs in the scope of initial planning, 3) understand the relationship of technology to the service to be provided, and 4) choose technology that will meet the mission and life expectancy needs of the library. This process insures that we understand that total cost includes the impact that all of our purchase decisions have on service.

This is an interesting perspective, that quality has both cost and customer service impact. It rules out the notion of saying that we can provide an inexpensive printer because we have decided in advance that users will just have to put up with any unfortunate design features. It means that the full cost of paper, ink, and support time will be accounted for in making decisions. And best of all, it looks at the whole picture. Rather than squeezing a purchase into the budget, we look at the way user and staff functions will be affected and make adjustments efficiently within the library budget.

DEFINING TOTAL COST

Assessing the cost, performance, and quality characteristics of technology is accomplished by first understanding the variables at work in defining cost, defining the performance characteristics needed to support user service, and then matching the characteristics of both. Quality judgment is then the primary variable in selecting the specific hardware and software that will meet the combined cost and performance characteristics.

Cost of technology is affected by:

- Equipment and software initial cost
- Security and adaptation costs
- Initial configuration costs
- Training overhead
- Ongoing support cost
- Proprietary constraints built into the systems
- Adaptability of the technology to new service needs

Let's examine each variable a little more:

Initial cost for technology is comprised of the actual cost of equipment and software, the staff time taken to research and specify what is to be purchased, initial supplies, and infrastructure connection costs such as network connections and electrical wiring.

Security and adaptation costs include anything that keeps hardware in place, safe to use, and free from tampering. For microcomputers this would typically include purchasing and installing security cables, security software to lock down the desktop and operating system, drive covers to secure CD drives, filtering software in children's areas, auditing software for licensing compliance, and virus protection. Adaptation is the provision of access software and hardware to accommodate a variety of disabilities, languages, and types of learners.

Initial configuration costs are those personnel and software expenditures required to connect systems to local area networks (LANs), to access centralized CD and Web-based databases, to set up printing systems, and to install management systems. More recently there has been a related need to create graphics, Web pages, and user instructions for desktop systems.

Training overhead is met in a variety of ways. Staff may choose to have formal training, do independent study, or attend workshops. Patrons may be required to meet technological literacy requirements, but libraries are rarely free of the need to provide over-the-shoulder and group orientation for patrons. Computer tutorials and help systems may also be useful in minimizing training costs.

Ongoing support costs include troubleshooting and repairs, spare parts, reconfiguration, backup of data and configuration files, and upgrades. Variables that affect support costs include maintainability, obsolescence, parts costs, and speed of repair.

Proprietary constraints built into the systems include the software driver compatibilities manufacturers provide, speed limitations that limit adaptation to new communication systems, compatibility of storage and printing devices and formats, and the hardware compatibility that affects interfaces inside the cabinet and with external systems.

Where adaptability of the technology to new service needs is required as new communications and software are introduced, computers may dramatically become obsolete. Strategies for minimizing impact of new standards and capabilities may include short-term strategies and replacement costs.

PERFORMANCE CHARACTERISTICS NEEDED

Patrons operate in an artificial environment within the library to the extent that they can access materials using database interfaces and retrieval rules devised by the library profession, vendors, and system designers. Generally, we expect that the majority of systems will have interfaces such that the user can walk up and begin using them immediately. Individual libraries may have users with rather different abilities to meet that expectation and systems that sometimes cannot meet the expectation of immediate use. In some libraries, patrons will be new immigrants who cannot, unassisted, immediately use a mouse or the Internet. Businessmen in some libraries may need to access the Bloomberg system but cannot do so without an hour or two to familiarize themselves with the system.

To analyze the technology needs of patrons takes the librarian outside of the comfort of current operations and may require considerable "what-iffing" to do a complete job. Some of the questions that might be asked include:

- Do users require remote access to library resources?
- Will the library be responsible for copyright in any situation?
- Will user orientation to new technology require new strategies and orientation materials?
- Will new technology change staff work flow?
- What kind of navigation aids will patrons require to find materials that are in a technological format as well as in print format?
- Do patrons need to print, download, or view materials?
- How many computers, printers, and other devices are needed to meet peak demand?
- To what degree can patrons be expected to use resources wisely?

PREPARING TO ACTUALLY ACQUIRE NEW TECHNOLOGY

Technology generally falls into one of four categories: state-of-the-art, less fully configured, name brand but outmoded, and cheap fully configured. (Minimally configured machines are not acceptable in an industrial environment, generally because we expect to be able to use computers as general purpose devices.)

The first of these generally is a name brand machine that includes the fastest processor available, a large fast hard disk, and a degree of quality that will provide the using organization with the longest life expectancy.

A less fully configured name brand computer may be something of a risk for upgrading, but if support and replacement are available it's a good choice for a five-year lifespan. Generally, machines configured for "home use" or "personal" use may have less standardized components.

Older name brand computers can provide reliability where complex tasks are minimal and greater reliability is needed, usually in applications areas such as word processing and support tasks.

A cheaper machine, usually a "clone" or less well-known brand, may be fully configured but is normally less well-integrated and may deliver less speed and efficiency as a result.

On the other hand, nothing in the quality process rules out making proper management decisions. It may be that some resources, even though they may be the least expensive, are too much of a risk in some other way. We may wish to use ink jet printers in public areas, for instance, and find that some of the models with the best features have parts that are too delicate or controls that are too complex for users.

GATHERING DATA

Information from the library now has to be gathered to build an estimate of life cycle costs.

Analyze library needs

Embarking on any systems improvement should be based on a clear understanding of the needs being met. All library staff should have an input into the needs assessment process because there will be parts of each person's work that must be included. Information should be in the form of specific abilities and tasks rather than just a wish list of hardware or software. A suggested form for needs assessment is provided in Appendix C. The form should probably be used in conjunction with observation by an experienced systems analyst or office process supervisor who can spot opportunities and solutions beyond the knowledge base of the staff.

Analyze candidate systems

Hardware and software features from a variety of sources need to be compared for both features and cost impact. Feature comparisons are relatively easy to acquire in popular magazines, but cost impact may require some fieldwork. Check computer stores and supply catalogs to obtain prices for the consumables such as ink cartridges for printers, floppy disks, backup tape cartridges, and cleaning supplies.

Part of each system chosen will include some items that stem from environmental, architectural, and ergonomic considerations. As systems are considered, it is important to relate the proposed systems to the current workspace to see where furniture, human movement spaces, and human working environments will have to be modified. As an example, lack of desktop space may dictate purchase of floor stands for some computers or purchase of tower configurations. Desktop height might dictate installation of keyboard trays. An employee with limited dexterity might dictate purchase of a trackball. Computer installation at the circulation desk may require a lower desk or taller seating to accommodate fatigue and access problems.

STAFF OUT IMPLEMENTATION OPTIONS

Impact of changes in the number of staff, their productivity, and their training can make an enormous difference, of course, in the costs associated with technology. Especially in first implementations, there is no track record to estimate whether there will be an impact. Libraries who have experienced their first use of computers know some of the possible impacts:

- Desktop publishing of library brochures, flyers, and posters becomes possible. Someone in the library develops these skills and it may consume 50 percent or more of one person's time.
- CD-ROM selection, acquisition, and update confronts the reference staff, taking perhaps 10 to 25 percent of one person's time, in addition to discussion time between reference staff.
- Training to use new or upgraded software can be done gradually and some will be a one-time experience as staff members become familiar with software and learn to generalize. First year training will probably take a week out of everyone's effective time. Far more important is allowing the flexibility to have some learning time built into daily activity.
- Users require more orientation to library resources because they must learn sufficient skills to manipulate databases, printers, the Internet, and computers that are used for access.

AMORTIZING FIXED COST

Purchase costs, initial software licenses, and other items that are purchased relatively infrequently may be amortized; i.e., purchase cost may be attributed to each year of the useable lifetime. Ideally, replacement costs will be programmed into budgets to pay for partial replacement of equipment in each succeeding year.

To amortize effectively, it is important to have a notion of what the life cycle should be for each type of item. Over the last 24 years some notions have emerged. Library systems vendors have suggested that the useful lifetime of integrated library systems is about seven years. Corporations tend to replace desktop microcomputers in a three-year cycle. Somewhere in that ballpark lies an approximation for most of us: between three and seven years. For microcomputers, my suggestion is to look at a five-year lifetime and for most printers the full seven years. A few items, such as CD-ROM drives, keyboards, and pointing devices are likely to come closer to the three-year lifetime.

Other factors will affect the useful lifetime of equipment. Public use computers will wear harder; small, personal laser printers will probably wear out faster in public service; and certain interface cards may be useful substantially longer than the machines in which they are installed. Software lifetime is determined by rather different factors.

Software will last as long as the intended use and the platform remain reasonably the same. For instance, a budgeting procedure set up in the early 1980s in Lotus 1–2–3 may be quite as viable today as previously, and the version of Lotus in use may be the same even though the user may have changed hardware at least once. Upgrades are to be expected in both applications software and operating systems, but the actual software used may span generations of hardware. The more likely reason for software upgrade will probably be a need for compatible drivers and new functions. Even if this amounts to software companies "churning" the market as some have charged, the cost of new drivers and functionality is at least a partially good justification.

Software will eventually require routine upgrade to remain suitable, but this cost will not be as great as going to completely different software. Upgrading will not require the investment in staff time that conversion to new software might. The cost of upgrade is really more analogous to maintenance cost in hardware and a much longer lifetime is reasonable to expect, perhaps as long as a dozen years. Most notably, personnel training cost is most likely to only require renewal, and quite a lot of self-growth is to be expected.

With a useable lifetime assigned to each element of the technology, the next step is to amortize the cost. What this means exactly will vary between organizations. At the least it should mean that the replacement and/or upgrade costs are programmed into the budget so that funds will be available at an appropriate moment to purchase new technology. Optimally, it would be desirable to have an equal division of the cost in each succeeding year with a plan to replace specific elements of technology each year. Since funds rarely carry over between budget years, some careful fitting of which items will be purchased must be expected to allow purchase of some of the more expensive items.

For equipment, the amount budgeted will be related to initial purchase price and will require matching the full initial investment amount by the end of the amortization period. Follow whatever local procedures are used to estimate for inflation, but it is unlikely that future costs will be less than original investment costs without a reduction in quality. Software costs should be estimated to be at least 10 percent of initial investment cost per year for upgrade.

EXTRAPOLATING VARIABLE COST

Include variable cost items in technology estimates or risk losing credibility with parent organizations. Variable costs include expendables such as paper and ink, maintenance costs, and accessory software such as type fonts. There is a strong temptation to overlook such costs in initially estimating the cost impact of such items and few organizations have procedures for examining them. It would be hard to take a planner to task for unforeseen changes in service levels, but planning new equipment without estimating some minimum amount of consumables is reprehensible.

Clearly some costs will change with experience and development of funding alternatives, but it is possible to at least establish a baseline for consumable items. Changes in variable cost due to volume of usage may also be accounted for by a strategy for funding:

- Account for variance as budget contingencies; i.e., set aside a sum in the budget to account for these and emergency costs. Such a fund can be converted to use for upgrades, purchase ahead, or acquisitions at the end of the budget year.
- Use cost recovery; i.e., charge users for at least part of these costs if a quality product can be consistently delivered.
- Pay for variable cost out of income that increases in some proportion that tends to match the rate of increase in the variable cost. An example would be to use copy machine income that increases with library usage.

ADJUSTING COSTS AND SYSTEMS TO MEET SPENDING GOALS

Fitting technology and cost to meet organizational goals requires applying the knowledge gained in data gathering about the organization and the desired systems. Ideally, someone with an understanding of both the professional area and technology should make the fit, but some guidelines will help most professionals make informed choices.

Some of the adjustment areas to look at should include:

Hardware

- Storage media in networked computers trades off between that which is available on each machine and that which is available in the network. Some minimum amount of local hard disk space is required to operate a workstation, particularly to buffer large graphics. The speed of a hard disk is very crucial in speeding the use of most graphic and Internet software. On the other hand, long-term storage may be more economically done on the server where routine backup of the data insures against loss. Networked storage space means that individual machines do not have to be equipped with backup tape drives and there is no need to train individual users to be reliable backup operators.
- Video monitors need to be large for users that do desktop publishing and other graphically intensive tasks. Increasingly, public access and service terminals need monitors larger than thirteen inches, but may do well with fifteen or seventeen inch units.
- Consider tower model computers for offices to minimize the purchase of ergonomic devices and keep desktops useable.
- Plan facilities and office layouts to allow sharing computers where shift workers make this a convenient option.
- Match the technology of standalone CD-ROMs to the generation of software used as a search engine. If you are still using a DOS-based application, a Pentium computer may be overkill. By the time you read this, most libraries will be in the process of using Web-based or Windows-based CD-ROMs.
- Trackballs require less frequent maintenance and have longer useful lifetimes than mice.
- Fewer printers need be purchased if several printers are hooked to many computers. One method to do this is to use a local area network. A local area network can operate a print server with one or more printers attached. Another approach is to have an automatic switchbox that can hook several computers to one printer and buffer the print jobs.

Software

- Look at functions to be performed and thoroughly investigate the capabilities of software you consider purchasing. Buy copies of technical software for people that really need them, but realize that minimal database, desktop publishing, and spreadsheet capabilities are now built into word processors.
- Consider file formats that data is required to be in for some purpose, whether to transfer to an OPAC system or to be uploaded to a Web page. Purchase software that can save data in those formats so that you don't end up purchasing additional software for data format conversion later on.

- Centralize less-used software, particularly graphics software, on one computer that everyone has access to.

Maintenance

- Choose a maintenance plan to replace broken units, have a support contract, have in-house repair capability, or use a vendor when items break. Document the plan and which type of equipment will be maintained in which fashion.
- Where maintenance costs are not invested at the beginning of the year, insure that some form of holdback or categorization is implemented to keep some funds available to cover emergencies.

BUDGETING

Technology should be realistically budgeted, with clear understanding about where each item in the technology plan is funded. A technology spending plan, even if not printed in the official budget, should be well documented. If a spending plan is not prepared and documented, it is quite likely that the ad hoc changes in purchasing decisions will make it difficult to meet library goals.

Within the budget, technology must be purchased within specific, appropriate categories. Libraries in educational institutions are particularly required to show how much is spent for library materials and overhead costs. Parent institutions and accrediting agencies track funds assigned to specific category codes, so the library should avoid skewing the budget with ad hoc budgeting. It may be time consuming, but make the budget transfers into appropriate categories to maintain accountability.

A technology plan should be linked to the budget. A sample of what goes into a technology plan is included in Appendix D. The purpose of a technology plan is to clearly link goals, technology purchases, and available resources so that there can be common effort toward goals.

DESIGN TO COST

When it comes to making decisions about technology spending, tradeoffs have to be made. The formal process of making those tradeoffs is probably best done in the framework of "design to cost." The philosophy of such a framework is simply that quality of either the organizational product (which may just be improved productivity or effectiveness) or the technology itself must not suffer in the process of designing or engineering the system of technology that is purchased and implemented. While it is easy to philosophize about design to cost, and management actions may seem well-intentioned, such a policy is

TEN STEPS FOR ESTIMATING INITIAL TECHNOLOGY COSTS

1. Choose a name-brand manufacturer for each type of item.
2. Get the most recently published estimates for new items from current publications.
3. Fully explore and choose all of the accessories and features needed.
4. Determine the time period within which the items will be purchased.
5. Apply an inflation factor estimated to occur between the present and the time period of the purchase.
6. Determine who will do installation and what the cost will be.
7. Determine the cost for electrical and network connections, furniture, and facilities changes.
8. Figure the cost of expendables, minor cable and equipment, and ergonomic devices.
9. Estimate the cost of maintenance.
10. Estimated cost is the total cost (items 6, 7, 8, and 9) times the inflation factor (item 5).

not a useful tool until it can be operationalized; that is, put into practice in a practical setting. Let's look at some of the possible ways cost might be constrained while still acquiring technology that will do a reputable job of meeting our goals.

The elements that are involved in designing a technology system that integrates well with the organization include cost, personnel, facilities, time, process constraints, and outcome deliverables.

Cost usually includes the outright cost of initial purchase as well as expected costs for upgrades, enhancements, and integration into network systems. Personnel include the support and training required for the technology. Facilities include the electrical and network infrastructure to accommodate the new computers as well as furniture, any unique server requirements, and building modifications.

Time involved in a system may include the time saved for portions of the organization that can obtain information more quickly, or the time saved by library staff in completing tasks or the training time that may be minimized by obtaining systems that require less training.

Process constraints include user printing needs, user access scheduling (are there peak demand times that will influence the amount of access?), accountability standards (must users login?), and reliability requirements (will less expensive systems lead to more "down" time?).

Outcome deliverables almost always include some textual or graphical document delivered to the end user, but may also include some degree of training, entertainment, e-mail access, services delivery from a remote resource (access to *Amazon.com* for instance), or research notes.

Adequately designing to cost requires involvement and brainstorming. The problems that are faced in designing to cost are exactly the problems managers and technicians are often tempted to ignore—people. NASA and other organizations have had problems listening to opinions and letting everyone in the organization who has a role with technology have their say. All the people involved need opportunities to think through the implications of changing the technology in use. Libraries are fortunate in that systems are generally small scale, but the need remains to spend focused time in committees and work groups considering all the ways new technology can be installed and used. The most useful way to accomplish the necessary brainstorming will vary, but it is sure to involve modeling activities that will get everyone thinking about the results. Some groups can do "what if" scenarios verbally. Other groups may do well to draw diagrams on a marker board, walk through the steps of procedures, layout location plans for equipment and wiring, or observe how tasks are done in other libraries.

Cost can be contained in ways that are largely independent of the specifications for the technology. These include varying the quality of computers purchased, changing the timing of purchases so that new equipment fits an upgrade cycle within the organization, and insuring lead time for staff to learn new software, thus minimizing impact on operations. Engineering to cost is a matter of spending the time to scope out the impact of cost decisions on operations so that the outcome is safe and has minimal impact on users.

SOFTWARE POLICY

Software policy constitutes both a tactical problem and a strategic problem. It's tactical in deciding what degree of access and type of software to provide patrons and staff, but strategic in responding to copyright needs and insuring that the library has the tools needed to carry out its mission.

DECIDE ON A SOFTWARE SUITE TO PURCHASE

The first decision that library management faces is which software to adopt. Along with that decision goes the need to determine where the software will be installed. Generally, a full software suite will be installed on staff computers to make word processing and other software generally available. Public area machines may need software too, but the decision will depend on the type of library. Applications software can provide access to documents stored on the Web and access to such documents is important to many users. The tradeoff of having word processing or other applications available to patrons may be unsatisfactory if it allows those functions to tie up computers when the library is heavily used. One alternative is to have a few machines set up for general purpose computing. Some libraries even operate such machines as a vended service. Another alternative is to lock down access to the software in such a manner that it only activates to support an Internet download.

MAINTAIN VERSION CONTROL

As new features are added, software companies provide the option to upgrade. Recently, the capability for vendors to update your software automatically has arrived. You may wish to disable such functions when you find them. For software versions and bug fix packages that are provided free, it is important to have a key individual or technician insure that the library computers are updated consistently. When the library begins to own more than two dozen computers, it may be worthwhile to have security software that is remotely administered and to have the capability to install software from a remote location.

GAMES

Probably governed by the type of library and the caliber of staff, a policy regarding games may or may not be required. Certainly most libraries will discourage game playing during duty hours.

WHO DOES INSTALLATIONS?

Technical staff or knowledgeable users should install software. This is a policy that seems trivial but needs to be clearly communicated to all staff members. Just as patrons need to be told not to place transparency material in copiers without permission (which can gum up the copier with burned plastic), so do staff need a real restraint on downloading and installing software of any type. The possibility of severely damaging productivity with inappropriate software or viruses is too great a risk. Does that mean staff can't have free screensavers? No, it just means that proper precautions need to be observed by having someone knowledgeable do the job and run a virus checker afterwards. Downloading software is different from downloading a graphics file to use as wallpaper. Neither a graphics file nor a plain text file is going to harbor viruses.

The real gray area in downloading comes with document files. Microsoft Word files have been notoriously infected with macro viruses. This really has humbugged academic organizations because faculty and students will author documents at home on a machine with poor virus protection and then load a document containing a virus to a Website or electronic course reserves where others download the document. The best protection in libraries is to have an up-to-date virus checker installed on every machine that can monitor downloads.

STANDARD SUBDIRECTORIES

Not every staff member maintains files to the same standard of security and tidiness. Confidential files such as personnel evaluations probably need to be kept on hard drives or floppy drives where access is not possible to routine browsing. Shared data such as bibliographic instruction files, databases, and reports need to be in relatively public shared drives on a network where everyone with proper security access can use them. Locating these files on network drives insures that documents which are repeatedly used are available during staff turn-over. Even if a malcontent should erase them, they should be available from network backups.

WHERE DEMOS ARE LOADED

A particular computer or disk drive needs to be reserved for demonstration software that is downloaded for evaluation. Such software should not be freely copied elsewhere, since that would risk copyright violation. Trying to decide what is licensed when users freely download trial versions is a major waste of technician time and makes configuration management a nightmare. Once staff have a chance to look at the software and decide that it is useful, the license can be paid and the software loaded on a regular staff machine.

SITE LICENSING

Purchasing a site license for all the machines in the library may be an economical way to purchase software. With budgetary considerations to make, it may not be possible to specify *when* a site license should be considered. What should be standard, however, is that site licensing should always be considered as a possibility in any software purchase.

USER-FLEXIBLE SOFTWARE

Where substantial ability for users to alter software exists, particularly in a networked environment, there should be some operational standard to insure library computers are available for duty. Such a policy should encompass requiring screen saver passwords, under what conditions users may apply word processor file encryption for sensitive documents, and who may set BIOS passwords.

SECURITY PASSWORDS

It's tough to please everyone and have security standards. Network and library system passwords should be protected. In most cases the technical staff will have responsibility for setting BIOS passwords. Both technical staff and some of the library staff should know passwords for the security software installed in the public area.

INTERFACES TO LIBRARY SYSTEMS SOFTWARE

Staff normally have individual logons to the library system. This is complicated in service locations where several staff members use the same computer over the course of the day. In most cases it is reasonable to require each user to logon as they assume use of the computer. That way security privileges are always set to the level of the user who has current access. Occasionally there may be situations where student workers need staff-level access and the rotation of students makes it inconvenient to have individual logins. In such cases dummy logins can be used to provide low-level access for routine duties such as circulation.

SHAREWARE

Downloaded software poses a challenge to computer security. Users should be routinely made aware that the library does not sanction unlicensed software use. Users who feel that a particular shareware would benefit their productivity should have access to a simple approval process, perhaps e-mailing the senior technician to seek permission to use a shareware product. The library should insist on proper licensing and record keeping to insure that management and technical staff are fully aware of the installed product. Perhaps the greatest danger is that the library might become dependent on software that it has little knowledge of, something that fails to get upgraded or that fails to transfer to a new computer. Even more importantly, tracking shareware will help provide a complete financial picture of the cost of doing business.

CONFIGURATION IN A LAN ENVIRONMENT

Who does what in a networked environment really depends upon level of expertise. Technicians should routinely have responsibility for network software installed on individual computers. At the same time, other proficient members of the staff may be responsible for setting up workstation configurations, backing up data, and installing printer and monitor drivers. Library staff particularly need to be able to rapidly open security on individual machines and change print location in order to facilitate unusual situations, such as assisting special visitors and the handicapped.

DATA EXCHANGE CAPABILITY

The extent that the library permits data exchange and recoding should be settled and made a uniform policy. Typically, users who correspond at great distances and those that have a need to transmit graphics may need to compress or encode files for transmission. Generally software to accomplish .zip or .tar compression or .uu encoding is inexpensive. Probably the greater worry is being sure that someone who meets the public, in either reference or circulation, is available to knowledgeably assist with such work without risking damage to the user's files.

WHO DOES TRAINING?

With all the software that may be in the library inventory, training can be a major issue. The person who conducts training needs, above all, to be a proficient user who understands not only the basic commands used by the majority of users, but the less-used commands that a professional word processor or manager will want to use. Whether the person selected is a technician, a library staffer, or a parent organization trainer, there needs to be a clear understanding as to what that person's responsibilities are. Training duties should not become that person's primary job without formally changing that person's job description. The person conducting training can very easily become the resource person for the entire staff. If that fits the person's role that's fine, but if it causes that person to become less productive, then the trainer needs to be supplemented with self-help training materials, a help desk resource, a technical guru in the organization, or some other source for routine user questions.

4 CHOOSING AND SUPPORTING APPLICATIONS SOFTWARE

CHOOSING SOFTWARE

Software comes in all kinds of amusing and interesting formats, most of them with an array of control buttons that would rival a control console on the *Starship Enterprise*. Once you see the first few advertisements and hark back to all you've ever heard about software, perhaps you'll remember a library school class or some other discussion about being an early adopter of technology. Should you purchase the newest word processor or shop around for an old standby that has a solid reputation? How does what you purchase relate to the life cycle costs for computing?

There are some guidelines to help make software purchasing decisions and they are based on a philosophy of helping users do what's best in the long term as well as the short term. My philosophy is based on the notion that users have a learning curve and will move from needing simple tools to requiring more sophisticated tools. Many software packages are simple enough for novice users to begin with and then grow in. Should a simpler package be acquired first and then a more advanced package? The best strategy to my way of thinking is to choose a software that will span the spectrum of learning, simply because users will learn a software then not want to give it up. If users lack readiness for computing in general or desktop/graphical interfaces, I would turn them loose on games, CD-ROMs, and e-mail to bridge their learning curve into productivity software rather than putting them into underpowered word processor and spreadsheet software.

GENERAL RULES THAT CAN GUIDE PURCHASING SOFTWARE

Choose software first, and then choose hardware. It helps immeasurably to know the software in order to make wise choices for hardware. With hardware decided upon first, you are locked in to fewer choices. Truthfully, you may have to decide on hardware and software together, but be sure you do your homework and become familiar with software if at all possible before you make a final hardware purchase. The limits that hardware are likely to impose are not related to brand but to CPU speed, disk space, hard disk seek time, and types of peripheral interfaces.

Consult reviews and become familiar with the functions that the particular type of software should be able to perform.

Choose software in the same generation of technology as the hardware and operating system you intend to purchase. This means checking to see what the most recent software versions are and what the optimum system is to run it on. Older versions of software should not be selected to run on a state-of-the-art system; newer applications should not be run on older computers. The graphics capabilities, disk drive capacities, overall speed, and amount of memory vary considerably between new and old computers. Software designers build software to an expected hardware environment.

Choose excellent single-function software for professional use rather than "all-in-one" programs that have several kinds of applications in one. The all-in-one type programs are things like WordPerfect Works and Microsoft Works, which will do word processing, spreadsheet, and database tasks but are fairly underpowered for professional use. These packages are different from "bundled" or "suites" of software such as WordPerfect Office, Microsoft Office, and Lotus SmartSuite where full-featured individual programs are provided that can be run independently from one another. There is a long history of multi-function software being generally less desirable and largely underpowered.

Be sure the software is compatible with the kind of printer, scanner, modem, or other peripheral device you wish to use it with. If you were purchasing software for home and it didn't work you could probably take it back. For professional-use software it's important to obtain specifications and be sure the software will be compatible in advance, rather than find it will not work after you've signed for the delivery of a dozen copies and the delay will impact the organization. A good source of specifications is the manufacturer's Website on the Internet complemented by reviews in magazines. Software drivers are usually found in software sold in the same "generation" as the hardware. If one is substantially older than the other there won't be compatible drivers.

Prefer software from companies that have been tried by the market place and survived. Microcomputers are no longer novel devices and it would be foolish to purchase software for professional use that will be risky to support and upgrade.

Prefer software that is highly rated by a public source like *PC Magazine* or *Library Technology Reports*. Utilize each source for its strengths. General purpose software reviews, for things like word processors, should come from popular magazines and reviews for library software should come from professional sources. If you can license software from state purchasing contracts there may be excellent price breaks for licenses.

Buy software from a reputable vendor in a full commercial shrink wrap package. In the past, unscrupulous vendors have packaged software with a computer and failed to provide certification of user rights or proper manuals. Even if software comes pre-installed on your computer's hard disk, you should purchase and receive a set of original installation disks or a CD and manual.

Choose software more for its functionality than its price. Less capable software can't grow with you. If cost is crucial, consider a mixed strategy of having a few copies of full-function software and many copies of a less-expensive software or an older version that can share files with the full-function version. You can then upgrade the less desirable package as your budget permits, but the staff can find a copy of the best software if they need a specific function or need to transfer a file to an outside agency in a newer format.

If the software doesn't come with a tutorial, consider purchasing one. Tutorials for most commercial software can be easily found as both computer-based training packages (CBTs) and as videos. Training materials empower people to learn the software when they cannot afford to be away from the worksite.

General purpose software is really marvelous stuff. Today you expect to find word processors that include a spell checker, a grammar checker, graphics, word art, the ability to do tables and charts, and layout capabilities that rival desktop publishing programs. So how do you decide between major programs of the same type? Several steps in the selection process are very much the same as the steps you go through in purchasing something for personal use, but for business purposes we need to be more formal and accountable:

- Check product reviews to compare specifications and prices.
- Discuss software with those who use or train in the software. Be careful to note obvious biases and probe enough to know if they are substantiated by actual software behavior.
- Look at the software yourself. There is no substitute for spending time with the software, checking it out. At the very least, choose a few basic formatting features and a few advanced features and try them out in each competing software.
- Checklist the features needed to do the tasks you have in mind, perhaps using the detailed charts provided in reviews so that you can be sure that functions that you need are present.

EXPERT USERS

Purchasing applications actually entails purchasing software for two different groups of staff members. People who have been using computers for a number of years have strong preferences for software. Rather than go through a campaign to maintain software purity, let me suggest a more constructive approach to keeping harmony in the family. Let professional staff and senior para-professionals choose the software they want to use. When they decide to use something that is not supported by the organization, have them sign the agreement given in Appendix E or obtain a verbal understanding that is equivalent.

WORD PROCESSING

Word processors are just about the most widely used type of general purpose software. The market seems at this point to be divided between two vendors, WordPerfect and Microsoft Word, with Lotus SmartSuite and Sun StarOffice as the spoilers. How do you decide if one of them or a new contender is best for your library? There is a hidden variable that must be considered, in addition to the users learning curve already alluded to, and it is simply the need to know word processing concepts. Word processing relies on features like proportionally spaced type, variable pitch fonts, hanging indent, tabs, line wrap, soft returns, and flush right. To adequately choose a good word processor requires that someone become familiar with those features and be prepared to appreciate how each software handles them.

Word-processing software should include a variety of essential features such as:

- Basic editing: cut and paste; copy; insert from file; go to; find; find and replace; and cut and save
- Basic formatting: left, right, and center justification; italics and bold; hanging indention; landscape and portrait printing
- Intermediate formatting: columns; tables; graphics; and outline
- Advanced formatting: graphics sizing; printer control of kerning and leading; line wrap across graphics; data fill; headers and footers; and left and right indent
- Mail/merge, sort, style sheet, and macros

DESKTOP PUBLISHING

Related to word processing, desktop publishing is a process for taking files created by a word processor and formatting them for publication. Formatting is termed "page layout" and treats text as an object, along with pictures, graphs, lines and other graphical items. Processing may not only include layout, but the treatment of the document for color separation for publishing, special effects like text overlaying graphics, and special text features such as curve fitting and warping. Desktop publishing packages pick up where word processors fail to function. For several years, for instance, the ability to place graphics accurately within text that was divided into columns has been a defining feature that desktop publishing software could do and word processors could not.

For library purposes, how much is invested in desktop publishing will depend to a large extent upon staffing and staff talents. Word processors are capable of constructing brochures, flyers, reports, bookmarks, bibliographies, signs, and other library publicity materials. Where production of extensive, artistically sensitive materials is needed and the investment can be justified, desktop publishing software may be introduced. A substantial cost in personnel training and production time is necessary, or hiring of a talented specialist who will be appropriately reimbursed is needed, to do effective desktop publication. If someone with computer talents is able to devote the time, as with any software, much can be learned by self-study.

Desktop publishing software spans a very large gamut of software. At the amateur level there are packages like Printshop and Microsoft Publisher that can produce a variety of useful brochures, flyers, and invitations. Printshop is fine for signs, greeting cards, posters, and simple materials. Microsoft Publisher is a step up into page design and would be a good program to purchase for all library staff to use. More advanced software like QuarkXPress and Adobe PageMaker can do all of the page layout tasks necessary for professional publishing.

GRAPHICS SOFTWARE

Along with desktop publishing there is a need for graphics to add the finishing touch to publications, presentations, and Web pages. Most computers can produce very elementary graphics with the Windows Paint program, but there is a need for something much more sophisticated. Packages like Super Paint and Corel Draw will allow some creativity with freehand and isometric drawing. Other software is available to do 3D perspectives, special surfaces, metallic textures, and other treatments. Software alone is insufficient to provide the range of graphics needed in most libraries, unless there is a graphics artist on staff. Graphics software must, therefore, encompass one or more clip art collections and access to collections of stock photos. One of the better ways to do that is to go to a provider that has a catalog or Web page presentation where unique stock photos can be acquired in small quantities. When purchasing clip art and stock photos be sure that the library receives rights to use them without a payment-per-use.

Two other sources of graphics are to have a scanner and a digital camera. Many libraries will have a scanner to facilitate interlibrary loan, and digital cameras are becoming very economical and of high resolution. Pictures of the library, people using the library, and the local environment are most effective in relating to patrons.

Scanning graphics into the computer requires not only a scanner, which usually comes with its own software, but an editing program like Adobe Photoshop. There is much more diversity in graphic software than possibly in any other area, so the task of choosing what is needed for your library may be a bit daunting. Recommendations of current software should come from authoritative magazines like *Desktop Publishing* and *PC Magazine*.

Some really basic characteristics of graphics software include:

- Tools—How difficult is it to select and use various features?
- Is there a capability to rotate a selection?
- Can drawings made up of multiple lines be decomposed to adjust or rearrange the lines?
- TWAIN Support—Will the program connect to a scanner for direct capture of images?
- Export Formats—Does the program support common graphic data formats, including bitmaps (.bmp), as well as .gif and .jpg?
- Internet Compatibility of Output—Are graphics easy to scale and save in .gif/.jpg format for use in Web pages?
- Resolution—Does the program utilize super VGA resolution (800 × 600 pixels) resolution or higher resolutions?

- Number of Colors—Can the program handle at least 256 colors or 8-bit color and preferably 24-bit color?

SPREADSHEETS

Choosing a good spreadsheet is another situation, like word processing, where there is a choice between a few principal competitors. Lotus held the lead and set the industry standard for years, providing a reliable spreadsheet that does calculation, graphs, and look-up databases. Microsoft entered the market with Excel that included good statistical functions and the ability to function in a graphical desktop. Because there are copyright restrictions on "look and feel" for software interfaces, the Microsoft interfaces are a bit clunkier than their rivals, but there are some good reasons for choosing either software. Add to this the other leading spreadsheet, Quattro, and the choice of a spreadsheet will be an interesting exercise.

Criteria for a suitable spreadsheet should include the following: Easy navigation to other parts of the spreadsheet with a minimum of keystrokes. Where possible, navigation should use the native PC keyboard to its fullest, cut and paste, including simple copy from one cell to many, copy one-to-many across rows and columns, and statistical functionality and ease of use for those functions.

GENERAL CHARACTERISTICS

Most applications software will share some general characteristics that you can look for that make using the software flexible and capable of adapting the organization to future opportunities.

The ability to read and save data in a variety of file formats is important. Even if the library is standardized on one software, outside agencies such as accrediting bodies, funding agencies, or vendors will end up having data you need to read in some other format.

Templates that are in a format for one particular document or computation provide shortcuts for users. Look for the number of templates available.

There should be a macro language that allows the software to be "programmed" to accommodate repetitive tasks. Word processors often have a macro language, the ability to create "styles" which are overall document formats that can be saved and reused, and "keyboard macros" which are simply a transcription of keys that the user presses to do a task and can be repeated on demand.

Wizards are fully constructed macros that step the user through a process. Look at the variety of wizards that are available and how much flexibility they offer in choosing outcome options.

Interaction with the user should include the ability to modify the command interface to place buttons and features bars where they best work for that individual user.

Maximum information and empowerment should be provided to the user, if and when they want it. Compare WordPerfect programs (that provide a miniature file manager whenever you open a file menu—you can print, delete a file, copy a file, etc., and file sizes are displayed) with Microsoft programs that simply open or close files with no ability to do data management tasks.

Help commands should be readily accessible and they should be thorough enough to cover how to use every command the software is capable of performing.

TRENDS IN SOFTWARE

Changing hardware and increasing user expectations continually push software authors to do more. Those expectations fit together with technical ability to create some long-term trends.

Software expands into the increasingly available disk space. Whether through poor programming practices or just sheer complexity, software takes up a significant amount of disk space.

Automatic features are replacing user choice with "guestimates" of what the user expects to happen. Fine control of word processors went out the window a few years ago. Word and WordPerfect make it all but impossible for users to go back to an environment where they control the format with simple direct commands. Staff capable of fully commanding the features of the software will continue to be rare and well paid.

The learning curve for advanced features is higher, as well as user expectations of what can be done. Users who can manipulate data, rather than merely enter it into software, and problem solve with the data continue to be scarce. Distinguishing levels of technical ability in staffing may give the library useful control of an important resource.

Ease of use enables novices to become productive immediately. Elementary features are available from menus and through "wizards," making it possible to do useful tasks with minimal familiarity.

Data is increasingly transportable between software from different developers. Partially this is the result of standards and partly the increasing expectations of users.

There is less emphasis on network functionality for word processors but much more need for databases to work in network and Web environments. Software may not have to be installed on a server and operated off the LAN—instead it can be installed on each computer. Increased disk space makes installation on each workstation feasible, and there are network utilities that make it possible to install software remotely, upgrade remotely, and assist users remotely. Software still must be capable of printing in a network environment and working with files on a network.

Web functionality, whether to communicate transparently over the Web or to format material for posting on the Web, is an increasing need. Library systems permit users to access the catalog via the Web and libraries provide other remote services such as interloan and database access to authorized users through the Web.

Use of the Web is increasing the awareness of formatting aesthetics. Users expect software to be more graphical, more interactive, and more object oriented. There continues to be frustration over the inability of applications software to move objects around as easily as icons can be moved in the Windows environment.

SUN recently released a "freeware" office suite called StarOffice. Whether it will survive as freeware is doubtful; one would suspect that upgrades will not be free. For cost savings, such introductory software may be an opportunity worth taking some risk.

PURCHASING SOFTWARE

ENVIRONMENT

Choosing software for the library may be affected by a variety of considerations that are imposed by the environment, and particularly by the parent agency. Among the considerations that may affect the library are the following:

Budget

If you have a flexible budget, you may be able to buy anything you deem worthwhile. Libraries that have a lot of discretion can often purchase unique software without justification. In more structured organizations it may be quite important to know when to justify items and when written justification can be bypassed.

Standards

Where the parent agency has decided upon standard software, you have to decide if standard software will do the job or whether it's worth extra effort to justify purchasing something else.

Compatibility

Not all software comes in a version to work with particular network operating systems, and sometimes a particular software package works exceptionally well with one particular operating system.

User preference

Some users may have a strong affinity for one software or a real distaste for another. Personally I prefer WordPerfect for word processing and would make a case for it, while someone else that has used Microsoft Word would fight for that program.

Productivity

Some software packages may be more productive because they are easier to use or because the package just happens to have a set of features needed for some of the work in a particular department.

Staff training

Library schools in the area may be training students in one particular type of software so that most local librarians turn out to have a strong preference for it. This may affect the level of training needed

PURCHASING PROCESS

Each organization has purchasing regulations that are intended to provide accountability, management information, and compliance with law. To step through the process with minimum effort requires doing the necessary homework to become familiar with the process and with the products to be purchased.

Become familiar with the market. You need brand names, prices, capabilities, and reviews of the current software. Computer magazines and library journals should be supplemented, if possible, with trips to computer stores, attendance at vendor fairs, slumming through displays at professional meetings, and seeing software that is at work in other workplaces. Software changes rather rapidly and it is very easy to inadvertently purchase an older version than intended.

Along with the information about products, you need to locate and know which vendor has the best price. Look for firms that advertise nationally or local stores that have consistently good prices. Within large organizations, check standing order arrangements and see if software is routinely licensed for the entire organization. Government libraries will need to check state and federal contract prices.

Understand the purchasing process. Within your organization there are purchasing rules that specify how much can be purchased from petty cash and at what amount you must bid out a purchase. There may be other possibilities; for instance, some organizations may limit petty cash to a small amount, perhaps $100, then they allow purchases up to $1000 by certifying that you have quotes from three vendors and have chosen the best price. Find out what documentation is needed for each procedure. As libraries add training rooms with many computers, knowing the purchasing break points will insure that you plan enough lead time when large software orders go out.

Avoid working the system. Going to bid is not easy, but avoid doing an end run by splitting orders to fit into less restrictive purchasing rules. It's one thing to be admonished by the Purchasing Office and quite another to end up caught short because the vendor can't figure out what it is that the library is trying to purchase on the split order.

Build good specifications. Even if you simply order software from a catalog, carefully written specifications are necessary to be sure that you get the version to go with the platform you are using.

Make the purchase order. Drafting a purchase order is a technical task that is rather different for software. Most organizations realize that there are no true "equivalents" and will only require competitive bids or multiple vendors for the identical item. Specify hardware that the software must be compatible with, including specific peripherals such as printers.

Receive the software and install the software. New software needs to be installed as quickly as possible so that it remains in warranty while you first start using it. New users may need to ask for assistance during installation and during the first month of use. Normally, a free support hot line may be available for the first month or two and then cost a substantial amount to use. Compatibility with other software and the hardware needs to be checked, of course, along with the need to obtain the correct printer drivers.

Take care of copyright and warranty. Send the warranty registration as soon as you have the shrink-wrap off the software. This will insure that you have access to support hot lines and that you receive notification of upgrades. Many vendors also provide access to libraries of screen and print drivers as well as interim releases of the software via the Internet. Complying with copyright is sometimes a complicated process, especially if the software is installed on a LAN. The primary obligation is to meet the product's licensing restrictions, which will either limit the number of simultaneous users or the number of computers on which the software is installed. Once you know the license restrictions, plan installation in such a manner that the library stays in compliance, regardless of the work requirements. In the case of LANs, this may mean obtaining monitoring software to insure compliance.

Purchasing usually requires some careful strategizing, particularly in a bid situation. First find out what discounts may be available. Many libraries qualify for educational pricing; others may find that there are discounts for purchasing a number of licenses.

SUPPORTING APPLICATIONS SOFTWARE

Over several years I've managed to meet a few people who have actually had to leave a job, or have rationalized leaving a job, because the employer required them to learn how to use software on their own and/or on their own time. I'm afraid that my sympathies have not been with them. In the broader scheme of things, everyone is in competition with someone else, whether that person is down the street or on the other side of the world. Learning new skills to increase productivity is an important aspect of the workplace. Ideally, employers should provide the means and the time on the job to do that learning, but in some situations it's just not possible. On the other hand, fast-moving organizations that cannot afford work time for learning often pay premium wages, which is an incentive in itself to do the learning on your own time. Even government agencies husband such an expectation.

In structuring the support we provide for software used by library staff and patrons, training is a major component. Most libraries are fairly accustomed to providing bibliographic instruction to patrons, including familiarization with the online catalog and database searching software. Less uniformity exists in how staff training is handled, largely influenced by the manner in which the library's parent organization handles training. The issue surfaces anew, however, as the library ascends the ladder of increasingly sophisticated technology. We begin to wonder whether the library is better off requiring new employees to be hired with appropriate technology skills or whether the library should train everyone, including staff already employed. Such issues are further complicated by the fact that most libraries don't keep staff training records. In a small library with perhaps six staff, such a record may be less necessary; but in larger organizations it may well become essential.

One approach to meeting the software support problem is to provide a thorough, well-funded, centrally supported training and advisory capability. In such a scenario, at least one staff member is responsible for all training needs. Their duties might include:

- Maintaining liaisons with software vendors to learn about upgrades, maintenance releases, and new products
- Providing expert advice on the use of specific commands and features as users problem solve while using the software
- Researching methods for completing unique tasks
- Coordinating software purchases
- Researching new software
- Conducting formal and informal training
- Devising local guides and standards for completing routine tasks with technology
- Scheduling training and updating training records

Another approach to meeting software support needs is to rely on individual staff members to learn applications through tutorials and by using the software. Some ways in which this might be facilitated include:

- Purchasing tutorial programs (CBTs—computer based training)
- Having one person be the "lead" person for each type of software
- Subscribing to a support service that will answer questions about several different applications
- Encouraging staff to take continuing education courses or attend professional association training sessions such as those provided through regional OCLC affiliates

Other options may exist, such as obtaining training and support through the parent organization, using a contractual service, or joining a consortium that provides training services.

With each approach to training and support, it is important to insure that the scheme you use for support and training includes:

- Initial training
- Daily support and problem solving
- Software upgrade procedures
- Software purchasing considerations
- Understanding new technological innovations that may require changing the type of software that is purchased

ISSUES

Among the issues that must be contended with in supporting software, some of the following are likely to surface: When should a new version of software be purchased? The best answer to this question is as soon after it is released as possible. If you waffle, think about: Does a competitive brand offer better features?

Whether to upgrade patrons or staff first will depend on whether users are likely to have the most recent software at home. If most of them do, they'll criticize the library if it lags in upgrading. Compatibility with clients is often cited as an important ingredient in business upgrades (Perkins, 1998).

Relate the upgrade decision to the hardware replacement schedule. Don't upgrade if the hardware is within 18 months of replacement. The version of operating system purchased with the next hardware cycle may well make other software more desirable. Consider upgrading a few machines as soon as possible. Invariably, a new scanner, digital camera, or printer will be purchased that will require software with newer features or drivers.

James Corbly has offered ten guidelines for deciding when to upgrade (Corbly, 1997):

- Printer drivers going out of date when you have newer printers
- Technical support from the vendor fading
- Too many workarounds developing
- Lack of macros and other improvements coming from the vendor or third parties
- Difficulty moving data to other important applications
- Decreasing compatibility with hardware
- Significant functionality in newer software
- The organization is going to a new operating system
- Newer software is acceptable to your library and to other libraries
- Hands-on experience with new software shows that it has favorable features and ease of use

IS A SITE LICENSE A BETTER DEAL THAN INDIVIDUAL COPIES?

Site license prices are frequently scaled by the number of units purchased, so the maximum discount requires a volume purchase. In such a situation it becomes useful to aggregate other people in the organization to buy in volume. Site licenses may remove some of the headaches in deciding which user stations or staff machines are to have the software.

Microsoft, back in 1997, moved to site licensing for educational organizations and away from "concurrent" licenses that are based on an average number of simultaneous users (Young, 1998). This angered users. Parent organizations, because of their size and staff expertise, are better equipped to deal with monolithic vendors like Microsoft.

MAY SOFTWARE BE USED ON HOME COMPUTERS?

Today, there are very few software companies that allow a copy of software to reside on a home machine. Most often, a license will allow an additional installation on a laptop with the proviso that only one copy be in use at the same time.

WHERE SHOULD THE LINE BE DRAWN BETWEEN DOING A TASK WITH IN-HOUSE SOFTWARE AND HAVING THE TASK DONE BY A VENDOR?

In-house work is best done when it is likely that only the library will have expertise to perform the task. Vendors can provide service when their overall cost is lower. Generally, for instance, a print shop can produce pamphlets from camera-ready copy less expensively than having library staff copy the brochures on a manually fed copier. (Use of a "mopier" printer that can duplex may provide low cost per copy and allow rapid production.)

SHOULD PATRONS HAVE ACCESS TO APPLICATIONS SOFTWARE?

In most libraries, applications software provides a service that users need, or assists with access to course reserves, or saves the time of users who are working in technical fields. Duplication of software installed on users' office machines or the machines of other public agencies is the primary consideration that would weigh against having applications software. Newer technology, perhaps a fax machine or a scanner with OCR capabilities, may provide a new service that the patrons value, cannot have on their office machines, and perhaps provides revenue that the library values.

AUTOMATIC UPGRADE

Letting the software upgrade itself is a new and potentially problematic situation with which to deal. Internet browsers and other software offer immediate upgrades when the vendor has them available. This can have devastating effects in some situations. Some integrated library systems, for instance, rely upon a standard browser installation. In other cases the databases accessed by the library through the Web may rely on a particular browser configuration that could be upset during an automatic upgrade. Although such situations can be explained to library staff, it may be wise to provide backup or security lock downs where high-turnover staff or volunteers could easily make a mistake by initiating an upgrade.

SOFTWARE IMPACT ON LIFE CYCLE COSTING

Keeping track of purchased software can minimize cost. By tracking software it is possible to know that each staff member has the ability to perform essential tasks. The greatest life cycle cost is in having poorly trained staff and staff without access to good software. The "opportunity costs" for diminishing staff capability and creativity far exceed the cost of software.

5 CHOOSING HARDWARE

CHOOSING HARDWARE

Overall, we purchase hardware for its power and reliability. Today everyone wants the "big iron" and every patron and staffer either knows the difference between crummy and good, or think they do. They may not be capable of filling out a purchase order, but they can make your life miserable if you purchase inappropriate technology. A bottom-line philosophy that has to apply to the purchase of hardware is to purchase as close to the state-of-the-art as you can afford.

One rule worth remembering was discussed with software: match hardware and software that you purchase so that they are in the same "generation." Installing the newest software, particularly new operating systems, on computers that are four or five years old is likely to cause problems with incorrect drivers and performance that doesn't meet your expectations. You are really purchasing what is known as a "platform"—some combination of hardware, operating system, and applications software that together provide the service that the user needs. What constitutes a platform in today's computer systems? Some of the following technology is involved:

THE COMPUTER

A central processing unit or "chip," which is the primary determinant of speed at which the system runs, as well as of many of the operating characteristics of the system is the core of the computer. Memory, which currently is high speed and very reliable, is also crucial.

A bus connects the CPU to peripherals, interface cards, and everything else in the system; the bus should also be as fast as possible. "Slots" for adding interface boards are attached to the bus, and the bus is part of the "motherboard" or main board that runs across the bottom of the case.

A monitor and interface card, which are their own computing system with independent memory, must be included. There are three types of disk storage: (1) some kind of removable disk that allows files to be physically transported, (2) a CD-ROM drive, and (3) a hard disk that provides storage of files, including the operating system and temporary data storage (buffering) during program execution.

THE OPERATING SYSTEM

Operating system software such as Windows, OS/2, or Unix is usually purchased at the same time as the computer. If the computer is a server, the operating system is likely to be a network operating system such as Novell or Unix. If the computer is a Web server, the operating system must be matched to the Web server software. The operating system provides most of the following:

- A graphical user interface (GUI) for user interaction with software
- File management capability, including backup, and subdirectory (folder) management
- Input and output with auxiliary devices such as mice, scanners, printers, plotters, and modems
- Support for applications software, including standardized setup and operation within the GUI

INITIAL PURCHASE

When purchasing computers for a first-time installation, there are several strategies that might be considered:

- Go for the least expensive systems available, with the notion that staff will take a while to appreciate speed and power
- Buy the best quality systems because they'll last longer and be more reliable
- Buy a mix of speed and quality to fit the tasks being done within the department the machine serves

While all three strategies have merit, the third is the most comprehensive. Some additional "best practices" might include the following:

- Purchase a nationally advertised brand that is well reviewed. Brand name is some assurance of quality and performance
- Obtain configurations that match particular tasks, but try to sort down to just a few main configurations for purchasing so that you rarely have unique configurations. The objective is never to have a "one-of-a-kind" machine that goes down for repair and cannot be replaced.
- Where the task is crucial, as with a server, be sure there is an identical machine in a much less-crucial task that can be swapped out and have a current backup ready to load

Examine what your idea of a "stripped" machine is. Vendors today sell machines with CD-ROM drives, sound cards, modems, bundled software, and removable media drives. A CD-ROM drive is essential, but modems are not needed if you are operating a LAN. You may decide other items such as sound cards are not essential on every computer. Work with vendors to get quotes for your version of stripped down systems. The number of computers may be an obvious factor but so is the variety of configurations. One way to leverage price is to see if the parent institution is buying a greater number of machines or has developed a relationship with a vendor due to a long-term pattern of purchases.

Look at where your OPAC system is in its life cycle. If you are going to have upgrades to a more graphically focused system in the next three years, consider buying machines that will be ready to support that system.

Initial purchasers of computer equipment face a diverse market. The predominant trends for corporate purchasers were recently documented in *Purchasing Magazine*. In their survey, 47 percent purchase through resellers, 34 percent purchase from manufacturers, and 19 percent purchase via the Internet (Avery, 1999). These are actually rather odd categorizations, since you can purchase direct from manufacturers via the Internet.

UPGRADING

Hardware is just plain difficult to upgrade. Typically, the closer to the top of the vendor's line the model is, the more likely it will be to have components, particularly CPUs, that can be upgraded. Invariably, if you upgrade hardware, there is a good chance that newer applications software will be needed and a newer version of the operating system will also be needed. An upgrade of the CPU chip is not all that goes into an upgrade. Usually the objective is to improve speed and performance. Just changing the CPU neglects at least two other important components: the hard drive and the memory. Ideally, the hard drive should be upgraded to a larger and faster model and the memory should double the existing memory. Keep an eye on bus speed as well. If the state-of-the-art introduces a new type of faster bus, consider strongly the option of buying totally new machines rather than upgrading. Since the bus is part of the motherboard, it tends to be unwieldy and uneconomical to replace.

Financially, there are tradeoffs to be made in upgrading hardware.

As part of a larger strategy it is probably wise to look at the cost of a new system. If an upgrade exceeds 60 percent of the cost of something new, consider the new machine. There are two elements that make a new machine a good choice. One is that there are likely to be new peripheral devices with a new machine that would not be part of an upgrade. Another element is the opportunity value of purchasing something new; in all likelihood, a new machine will be more reliable and it will likely have a longer life cycle than an upgraded machine.

SHOULD THE LIBRARY PURCHASE MACINTOSHES?

The decision to purchase Macintoshes has two parts to it. The first consideration is whether the online public access catalog (OPAC) system will be compatible with Macs. The next consideration is whether there is a user audience that would prefer or benefit from Macs. Choosing user computers for the library is not done in isolation. If the majority of parent organization users have Macs, then it might be a wise choice for the library.

There are a few online library systems that are based on Macintosh servers. Such a system would be a first choice for small libraries where a uniform Macintosh environment is established for most users.

Where the OPAC is based on a Unix or other platform, Macs will work quite well for user terminals. The user terminals will have to be networked using a networking protocol such as Ethernet that will work with both computer types.

In choosing Macs versus PCs, the library should not be misled by claims of inherent superiority for either type. Benchmark speeds for processors and tasks are usually more than offset by real-world operating speed of individual software packages and by the other hardware harnessed in the same machine. Manufacturers are not motivated to make the process of comparing performance any easier.

Overall, the choice of using Macintoshes or Intel machines is going to be subject to the same parameters. What can the organization afford? Is the machine being purchased going to have enough useable lifetime and expansion capability to have a long service life? Will the components, particularly video cards, have enough capability to handle the tasks users demand of them? Will support staff be hired that have sufficient knowledge of Macs to assist users and troubleshoot problems?

SHOULD THE LIBRARY PURCHASE THIN-CLIENTS?

Thin-clients, computers that lack disk drives, are essentially intelligent terminals which seem to offer an advantage in being more impervious to viruses and less expensive to operate. Whether such machines will work in a library setting, where vendor products are somewhat prosaically dependent on standard computer configurations, is questionable.

The answer to this question may be decided mostly by the size and capabilities of the parent organization. To undertake setting up thin-clients takes some initial investment in technological know-how. If that talent is in place, the library can take advantage of it. If the talent does not exist, the library will have to take on a somewhat risky project.

In general, thin-clients might work best for staff workstations that are confined to accessing the library system and doing routine tasks such as serials check-in. Even in this role their capabilities are limiting since staff need to occasionally do projects with graphics, Web authoring, file transfer to diskette, and Internet access. If the parent organization already has some thin-clients it can't hurt to keep one or two, but they will not work as the mainstay of the library's computing needs.

WORKING WITH VENDORS

SPREAD BRAND NAME PURCHASES AROUND

Purchasing departments will go to different vendors to compare pricing for the same item. The state or parent agency may offer blanket purchase agreements with major vendors. It is still up to the library to determine if using one or multiple brands is a good way to proceed. The obvious advantage of using one brand is that repair technicians get used to one vendor's way of doing business. The downside is that a single vendor may not offer the particular accessories and peripherals that the library needs. Some large organizations rotate between brands to discourage computer manufacturers from offering proprietary—i.e., "closed"—systems.

PURCHASE FROM MAINSTREAM BRANDS

Although there are a number of reputable generic computer manufacturers, only top vendors put effort into integrating components to

IMPORTANT FACTORS WHEN WORKING WTH VENDORS

SERVICE CONTRACTS

What kind of service contract would work for the library? Most computers are sold with an initial service contract for parts and labor, covering the machine itself for a term of one to three years. An extended warranty with similar terms is usually available. If the contract is part of the purchase cost of the computer, be sure before you purchase the extended service contract that the service contract will fit the total picture of library support.

A typical service contract provides for maintaining the hardware. How are day-to-day minor tasks to be handled? If a floppy disk is stuck in a drive or a keyboard develops a bad space key, who takes care of it? If the staff secretary needs help with a word-processing program, can she call someone for help? If the virus-detection program finds a virus, can the library staff handle it? When a staff member leaves the organization, is there someone who can clean old files off that computer's hard disk without ruining the operating system? Is it possible to contract support for servers and telecommunications gear?

To choose service contract support, the first step is to define what the library needs. Once you can define the range of tasks required, choose support agencies that can provide the needed services. Chances are that the extra services, such as providing help desk support for ad hoc questions, support for applications software, or help with risky problems like viruses, will cost extra and may require a separate contract. In general, it is a poor decision to try replacing some minimum amount of technical staff with a contract.

Watch out for per-minute call charges for telephone support. A per call fee is one thing, but chatty or needy staff can run up the bill on a minute-by-minute service.

Also pay attention to service area definitions. If the library is out of the main service area you may be paying mileage charges.

Carefully read the covered equipment definitions. You need the equipment covered, but with today's complex operating systems you may need help figuring out whether you have a hardware or a software problem. If the contract is too tightly defined you may not be supported.

Technicians at local companies, in particular, can be very wonderful or very poor. Choose a local company on reputation, performance guarantees, and personal interviews with the actual service staff.

PURCHASE NEGOTIATIONS

Several factors influence the price you will pay for computers: purchase volume, configuration, and perception of future sales potential. Obviously, if the library can aggregate orders with other parent institution units it will be a larger order and provide room for a larger discount. The more diversity there is in configuration, the less the seller can discount. To keep configurations simple, it may be better to dress up some of the computers to have a few extra disk drives and other components than to move all the computers to less-extensive configurations. This approach may be better because the factory-installed components have better reliability, the added features may extend the equipment work life and give the library more flexibility, and the discount on the simplified order will help pay for the added items.

Negotiating for discounts is done best by knowing the vendor's product and having a computer-knowledgeable staff member contacting the vendor. Prices and configuration are usually published on the Web and in magazine ads. It is very useful to combine the task of getting clarifications about technical features and compatibility with the task of asking the best price on a particular configuration. Part of getting a good price is being a good customer. A good customer knows when to ask questions, is concise, and uses one contact person.

Expect good discounts that are at least 10 percent of the order price. Don't expect a great discount on pre-configured "state contract" configurations unless you are making a substantial order, perhaps more than 50 units. Those prepared configurations are usually set up to be easy buys. Examine "educational" configurations carefully to see if they are state-of-the-art and have comparable features. They're not bad purchases, but the buyer should be aware that they may end up trading flexibility in choosing options for a good price.

In some organizations you may have to take bids. Most of the negotiating power will be in making tradeoffs between vendors. You may wish to have the vendor install the computers, for instance, or to install and configure basic software. If those options are separate line items in the bid, you can distinguish which vendors will provide the services you need. Use bid conferences to clarify aspects of each vendor's submission.

LEASE VS. PURCHASE?

It is rare to find a reasonable way to lease computers for what is really an industrial setting like a library. Two factors reason against it: high wear rates on the equipment and rapid obsolescence. It is extremely hard to insure that what seems like a reasonable price for leasing a competitive machine will seem like a reasonable price in 18 months. The leaser hopes that at the end of the term the computers leased will retain enough resale value to net some of the initial purchase cost upon resale. Other strategies may play in as well: The leaser may provide machines that are just a little behind the state-of-the-art so that the "glitz" cost has already ebbed.

Leases would seem to be most viable in smaller organizations that need fewer than 20 computers. Libraries in out-of-the-way locations may also be well served to lease. The primary tradeoff is that the library is spared the cost of hiring a technician.

Beyond the immediate problems of service costs, leasing computers might be compared to leasing a car. Would you lease a car? Could you limit your usage and wear on the computers to the limits in the contract or would you end up paying pro-rata service fees? Could you afford a down payment on the lease? Could you afford a balloon payment at the end of the lease if you wished to own the computers or terminate the lease?

NON-NAME-BRAND MACHINES?

Clones seem to be a good deal at the prices they are offered. Can the library live with the performance of a carefully selected fleet of clone computers? In all probability it can.

Computers are sold in varying ways. Original equipment manufacturers (OEMs) sell through name brands and put effort into customization of the final product. Non-name-brand "clone" manufacturers may put together generic components and the machines may be sold in large commodity lots through wholesalers.

Performance may vary considerably and you may well ask a few important questions:

- Can the machines match well-known benchmark tests such as those used by *PC Magazine*?
- Is there a warranty that will provide full or partial replacement?
- Does the manufacturer provide local service or is it provided through some other company?
- Is the seller a reputable company or simply an intermediary dealing in wholesale lots?
- Is the equipment composed of all new parts?

As these questions point out, most of the concerns with non-name-brand computers have to do with reliability and maintainability. Where the first thought about clones is that their performance may be slightly below the range of name-brand machines, even more thought needs to be given to the amount of added value name-brand companies put into their products. However, if you can obtain parts through the vendor, if there is a reasonable warranty period, and if there is good compatibility with other computers, consider purchasing clones.

USED/REFURBISHED MACHINES?

If you do not investigate the source of used machines, you deserve what you get. Greed for great prices and cupidity in buying "real name-brand computers" has clouded the mind of more than one technology manager. Investigating the source is important, whether inside or outside the parent organization. Hand-me-downs within the organization may be quite reputable. You can imagine, for instance, that a CAD lab or animation unit would need the fastest machines on the market and would hand over really capable machines as hand-me-downs. There are fewer chances that the accounting department will hand over near state-of-the-art computers.

What you really do not want to have happen is for the seller to deliver a "load" of computers to your facility in a pickup truck, have them signed for, and leave. Anyone who goes to computer fairs can provide about that level of service. The seller should provide reputable equipment with a full set of cabling, an installed and licensed operating system, and a minimum warranty for, say, 90 days. If you have a local dealer, they should be willing to help you set the computers up.

How much you pay for refurbished computers will depend on the market and the options the machines have installed. Check local computer newspapers and magazines to find "bluebook" prices. Shop around and compare prices with state-of-the-art machines that are available. Be prepared to pay extra for additional disk drives, larger memory, and faster clock speeds. Used computers, refurbished by the manufacturing company, are some of the best deals you can get. Coupled with a good maintenance contract, refurbished machines can have an excellent serviceable life in the library.

achieve higher levels of system performance. It is important to read reviews to obtain a sense of how much performance difference there might be between a major name brand and a generic brand.

Buy early enough to have room to maneuver. Vendors are well aware of budget cycles. When you place orders, try to do so early enough in the budget year so that you can cancel an order and buy from another vendor. This keeps vendors, particularly small local vendors, from supplying you with last year's model and charging you full price.

Buy early in the product life cycle. It's hard to find a name brand machine being offered that is more than two years old in the development cycle, but some vendors will continue to offer older models at incredible prices.

Aggregate orders with other parts of the organization or within library consortia to obtain the best prices.

FEATURES TO LOOK FOR

ERGONOMICS

Computers have several features which enhance access by those with disabilities. These should be available on any machine purchased. There should be software, usually part of the operating system, that makes it possible to use single keystrokes to give commands. There should be utility software that makes it possible to magnify portions of the screen. For staff that use keyboards continuously in their work, ergonomic keyboards that support palms and are pitched forward should be considered.

Privacy and ergonomics may team up in the library. Placing computers in desks with the monitor below the surface of the desk allows much greater patron privacy. Great care must be taken in obtaining such desks since there are some poorly made units on the market that require the user to assume aggressively uncomfortable positions to see the monitor.

INTEGRATION

More capabilities are being added to the motherboard. Currently, network interfaces, particularly Ethernet, and video interfaces are being built onto the motherboard of some models. In the past, when motherboards were relatively unreliable, this would not have been a good feature. In today's technology it represents a definite improvement in reliability and speed of operation.

QUALITY

Obtaining a "quality" computer is a matter of perception. Ideally it should be a unit composed of name-brand components integrated as a system that is optimized for performance with the operating system the library is using. When *PC Magazine* and some others review machines, they use benchmarks or standards that compare how machines function using a particular operating system—usually Microsoft Windows—and consequently machines which do well with Windows are more highly rated. Network machines are tested with Microsoft and Novell and perhaps Unix operating systems. Check ratings and be sure you understand which operating systems the hardware works best with. Another way of looking at quality is to be sure that the system is from a reputable dealer who will assure maintenance and parts replacement for three years or more. National brands win their place in the sun by making systems that are constructed with components that work well together.

MAINTAINABILITY

Vendors in the past have devised cumbersome mechanisms to make it difficult to open the case of the computer, have used means of attaching components that require special tools to remove and replace them, and have manufactured components that are physically incompatible with any other vendor's equipment. It is important to pay attention to these issues either by reading reviews or by having a technician address them in the purchasing process. The consequences of poor maintainability are that expensive special tools may be required and repair time extended because only technicians with skills to handle the special tools can do the repairs. There is also the possibility that only parts from the manufacturer will work with the computers.

SECURITY

Does the computer case lock or have a hasp for applying a padlock or security cable? Computers are often the target of petty pilferage of memory and other components and certainly may be stolen as intact units. Each machine needs to be locked to prevent tampering and to be capable of being locked to the furniture it is located upon.

SCANNERS AND GRAPHIC INPUT DEVICES

A scanner and digital camera are needed for Web authoring, but the scanner is an important device for interlibrary loan and for user access to some documents. With just a moderately priced scanner, most libraries can participate in electronic document transmissions to serve interloan via e-mail. More complex systems are needlessly expensive. A very small amount of expertise is needed to understand the use of various graphic formats, choose the correct one for a given situation, and use the scanner to make documents rapidly available. Basic criteria for scanner selection should include resolution, size of document that can be scanned, type of interfaces to the computer, and durability. For digital cameras, the quality of pictures and the number that can be stored in the camera are paramount. Increasingly, the convenience of setting camera controls and the ease of transporting the images are important.

CD-ROMS

CD-ROMs are a standard part of a modern computer and are required for installing most software. Currently available CD-ROM drives are high speed (40 × or better) and do double duty if they come equipped with DVD technology.

One or more of the staff machines in the support area should be equipped with a writeable CD drive (colloquially termed a "ROM burner"), which gives a great deal of flexibility for doing data backup and for configuring public area workstations. With the configuration of one public area workstation recorded on disk, all the machines can have an identical configuration copied to their hard disks in a very short time. If a user messes up a machine or something goes awry during upgrade you can restore the machine configuration in about ten minutes.

DOCKING STATIONS

Docking stations, where a laptop can be hooked into a fixed monitor, network interface, printer, and other peripherals, provide the flexibility that a bibliographic instruction specialist or library director may need. With a docking station to provide desktop utilization, laptops can provide staff with the ability to take a portable projector and do publicity presentations, training, or speaking engagements on behalf of the library. Every library today, with the need to demonstrate electronic resources, should consider having two laptops (one for service, one backup).

MICE, TRACKBALLS, AND POINTING DEVICES

Pointing devices are available in greater variety than ever before. Access for the disabled will be enhanced for some if there are a few high-quality trackballs available for patrons with limited motor control. A much wider variety of pointing devices is available for minimal cost today, so there should be enough economic flexibility to permit choosing a mixture and even experimenting with user preferences.

FAX-MODEMS

Fax-modems are often offered as standard equipment for home-use computer systems. Current professional practice is to offer Internet access to databases because it is substantially faster, so there is little call to use modems in a modern library. Fax modems are excellent accessories for laptop computers that are used outside the library. Greater autonomy and flexibility for laptops is possible with modems that contain or operate through a cell phone. If the library serves community groups with training and presentations in unprepared sites, a cell phone/modem is most useful.

MMX-COMPATIBLE (MULTI-MEDIA) MACHINES

MMX-compatible computers offer CPU and graphics features to handle full-motion video, stereo sound, and the newest Internet graphics and are a reasonable investment. Academic organizations may wish to assess the possibility of providing a lot more multimedia via computers than has ever been possible in the past. The advent of inexpensive DVD drives makes it worth considering whether educational materials in that format may be better than videotapes.

WHEN TO UPGRADE

Upgrade when there is no option for purchase. Such situations might occur, for instance, when grant money does not provide for purchase of new systems, only upgrades. It may be useful to upgrade for some particular capability; for example, in academic libraries going to electronic course reserves, it might be important to purchase seventeen-inch monitors to display documents.

Motherboards are the most difficult item to upgrade, but accelerator cards from reputable manufacturers make increasing CPU speed quite possible. Additional memory is an important investment that is increasingly affordable. Replacing a hard drive will increase access speed, but may require purchase of a new controller card as well.

BACKUP

Three major options are available for system backup: 1) backup to the LAN server, 2) backup to a DAT tape, and 3) backup to a writeable CD-ROM. The first option should only be used for temporarily holding data while a workstation is replaced or in an emergency. Tape drives and CDs are the hard-working backbone of backup systems and should be considered for servers and a very few key workstations where library reports such as inventories are run. For public area computers, backup of the initial installation should be done with "image" backup software like Ghost and written onto a WORM or rewriteable CD. This not only gives security from system failure, but allows restoration of a system in about ten minutes should a machine suffer from a hacker or virus attack.

A fourth backup option exists that is much more of a security precaution than true backup. With today's large hard drives it is feasible to backup to a second partition on the drive so that a computer can quickly be restored to its factory configuration. This is a suitable backup to protect against hacker attacks but does not help if there is a drive failure.

In some libraries, particularly where the library performs data processing tasks, document indexing, or graphics work, it may be useful to consider a hierarchical storage management system (HSM). Such a system uses software on the server that can automatically move data to less-expensive backup media as it becomes accessed less often. Users can still access the data, usually with a slightly increased delay.

Avoid entanglements. If something sounds too complicated, think about its impact on troubleshooting. A good example is a backup device that uses the printer port. Keeping such a device configured and troubleshooting which device is having problems is complicated by the fact that two devices are connected through one port.

INITIAL TROUBLESHOOTING

The vendor normally sets up a computer with the operating system already installed and the machine has been at least shown to be functioning. Users are then responsible for installing additional accessory cards, attaching and configuring printers, and attaching the computer to a network. The most likely problem encountered in initial setup is likely to be either an address conflict between components or an incompatibility caused by ordering the wrong item. Routine problems that occur need some basic user-level troubleshooting. Before doing more than light troubleshooting, it would be wise to know the extent of troubleshooting expected and sanctioned by your support agency.

Place an "out of order" sign on the problem unit immediately as a convenience to users and to protect the equipment. Ask the most recent user to describe problems they encountered. Reboot the machine. Note any error messages that appear and obtain screen prints if possible (**Prt Scrn** key in Windows, then paste into the Notepad).

The normal first thought in troubleshooting is to check to see that all the cables and electric cords are plugged in snug. Check to see if any front or rear panel LED operational lights are on which might give a clue as to what components have failed.

The next step in troubleshooting is to determine if a component that is causing the problem can be isolated. Swapping monitors, interface cards, cables, and other parts with existing systems may help isolate the problem.

Keep it simple. Before you go probing around for a stuck diskette or diskette shutter, for instance, it may be wise to simply turn the power off then upend the unit to see if the diskette part will fall out.

In public area machines, turn the security software off during troubleshooting, since that may inhibit proper error messages or system self analysis.

Check the vendor Website for problems that other users have encountered similar to the one you are experiencing. Vendors usually post bulletins to assist with troubleshooting.

Find a troubleshooting Web page like TipWorld or Ziff's where you can get ideas to assist with problem solving.

VENDING SYSTEMS

In almost every library environment there is now some kind of vending, whether it is copiers, pencils, printing, or typewriter use. Over the last few years, as Internet printing has increased, the need to at least control the amount of printing has increased in most libraries.

Pay-for-print has not been a technological challenge in most cases, but it certainly is a purchasing and management issue. The first problem that arises is that many libraries do not wish to handle cash and they do not want to have patrons queued up waiting for limited library staff. The solution is to have pay-for-print systems, whether on microfilm readers or networked computers, that are paid for using vending cards or coins. Such a requirement may be met using either a manual or computer-controlled system.

There are manually controlled pay-for-print systems. One such system is simply to have a standalone terminal with an attached printer where a patron can bring a floppy disk and print its contents. Another is to use a Novell network with Windows where printer drivers are set up with a user-level hold. When patrons print, jobs go into the queue but are held. Staff can then release the user block when the user is prepared to pay for the output. Security software is required on the workstation to keep patrons from changing the block function.

Among the best options is a computer-controlled printing system that can meter printing while keeping statistics about use. One approach that is often suggested is simply to put a coin-op device or card reader on each machine. Using a payment device per workstation is extremely limiting, however, should there be a need to connect a group of new computers.

Several companies offer very useable print payment systems, but they are in transition. The best software is currently vended through small vendors who require the library to purchase the print management system. They are not capitalized to implement a vendor-owned printing system. The market is made more complex by the advent of large companies that are entering into the enterprise-wide vending business. Such companies can institute payment systems for all the devices, from Coke machines to microfilm readers, throughout the organization. Unfortunately, these larger firms as yet have almost no expertise in implementing self-service printing management. If the parent organization or a large library were facing the prospect of implementing such a system, they would be wise to allow vendor alliances to deliver pay-for-print systems.

The following basic cost model is based upon parameters that became evident while investigating and implementing a real world pay-for-print solution. Where possible, assumptions and scaling factors are identified. Users should apply care in developing a total-cost-of-ownership model of their own, realizing that institutional culture, physical facilities, and user behavior may vary considerably. Pay-for-print solutions vary considerably in their topology and constituent parts.

In each system there must be at least one central computer that is

Placing a printer at each workstation is not desirable because there are then more machines to be maintained and usually the smaller printers are slower, usually provide poorer print quality, and are usually less durable. Larger printers can duplex and print at high speed.

TABLE 1—PRINTING MANAGEMENT OPTIONS					
	Manual system using cash or paper cash card at the front desk	Manual system with card reader not connected with the printing system	Payment card reader per workstation	Combination central payment and print stations	Central payment station, Print station
Staffing required?	YES	YES	NO	NO	NO
Prevents excessive printing?	Depends*	Depends*	NO	NO	NO
Easy to scale up?	NO	NO	NO	YES	YES
Intuitive for students?	YES	YES	Higher	Medium	Medium
Multiple printers?	YES	YES	NO	YES	YES
* Manual systems depend upon the network operating system to provide metering. If the operating system can honor a user print hold from the user's computer and if it can provide staff the capability to override the hold (which the combination of Novell Netware and Windows does) then these systems can prevent printing waste. The print job is held in the print queue until a staff member releases the hold.					

used with installed software to operate the pay-for-print software and spool print jobs to the printer. That computer must be reasonably current for operation while attached to the LAN but does not have to be absolutely "state of the art." More importantly, because this is a public access computer, it must be capable of being locked down by the security software in use by the library. Software for pay-for-print output metering varies according to the pricing strategy of the vendor. A small-scale application of 30 computers may cost as little as $1,800 or as much as $6,500. The software of course varies to match the price, from fairly simple capability to print when the job is paid for all the way to feature-rich programs that can have multiple payment modes, several user categories, courtesy copy override, touch screens, and statistical analysis.

Support for pay-for-print varies considerably, but has one common characteristic. Initial field-level troubleshooting will be performed either by the library's staff, by vendor staff, or by both. To that extent, the cost is a sunk cost or a minimally incremental cost. In the same way, technical assistance during installation costs may be a sunk or minimal cost. The major expenses are the costs of replacing a com-

TABLE—2 COST FOR A PAY-PER-PRINT SOLUTION	
Computer	$1,400.00
Print management software	$4,500.00
Table(s) for computer and printer	$600.00
Printer	$800.00
Network drop	$100.00
Total	$7,400.00

ponent, having a specialist make adjustments, or having offsite repairs performed. Given that individual instances can vary considerably, an annual average cost of $1,000 is suggested. It would be wise to have these funds actually become part of the institution's repair fund to accommodate the variability in cost. Upgrade of the pay-for-print software is a real consideration and should become part of repair cycle cost, if possible. If separately accounted for, an initial increment of $500 is suggested for the first "out year" of the life cycle with tri-annual increments from there. Increments should be scaled according to estimated upgrade costs provided by the software vendor.

CONSUMABLES

An additional cost to many pay-for-print projects is the cost of providing payment cards for the system. Several options, and therefore decisions, exist. Payment cards may be based on a magnetic strip already in place on patron ID cards, it may be based on a separate copier or printing card, or it may be that the user has a bar code on an ID card that is keyed to a deposit payment system. The following table summarizes some of the most important expenses that may be involved:

TABLE 3—CONSUMABLE COST ESTIMATES	
Paper—1 year (1 box paper = $50.00)	$300.00
Toner—1 year (1 toner cartridge = $120.00)	$360.00
Mag-strip cards (cards cost $.50 each)	$2,500.00

ACCESSORY HARDWARE

Beyond the immediate server and printer hardware are a number of items that are needed to complete a system. Each system may or may not need these items. Typical costs are listed here for a small 30-computer installation. Scaling and differences in vendor products and packaging may make for significant differences in this area.

TABLE 4—ACCESSORY HARDWARE COST ESTIMATES	
Coin-op mechanism	$1,300.00
Magnetic strip reader	$1,500.00
Encoding hardware for magnetic strips	$1,600.00
Change machine	$1,000.00

When estimating costs for the operation of a pay-for-print system it is important to reach the bottom line and estimate the break-even point. It is possible to estimate a break-even point only by having some reasonable idea of the volume of printing that will be done. Estimates based upon print experience, while printing is done free of charge, are poor indicators. It is most important to obtain realistic data, even if that requires operating a payment system with manual intervention, such as placing the printer behind the circulation counter for a short period of time. Once an estimate of print volume is available it is possible to summarize installation and first year costs, accessory equipment costs, and consumables costs. Each cost category has to be estimated for actual vendor/local pricing, number of patrons served, print volume, and local environmental conditions. The first year data can then be averaged with second and third year costs and divided by the annual copy volume to obtain an idea of how much cost must be recovered in per-page charges. The break-even point is the point where the number of copies is exactly the number estimated when setting the per-page charge. Advertising, volume discounting, increased user population, and other factors may alter costs or the volume of use.

HARDWARE TRENDS

The advent of palm-size computers and electronic book readers opens the door further to situations where the library acts as a facilitator. Already a number of institutions are offering Ethernet connections for laptop computers. The smaller hand-held devices are likely to expand the number of people who are able to afford access and change the economics of information transfer (Hardin and Ziebarth, 1998). Libraries will be challenged to provide access for a wider variety of transportable devices. Two associated developments are likely to make palm and laptop computers a key element in library services. One is the development of a special typeface for electronic books by Microsoft. Another is the advent of wireless radio frequency and infrared connections between Ethernet cards in the computer and network interfaces made available for public connection.

Inexpensive color devices, printers, scanners, and good digital cameras are making it harder to determine where to draw the lines around what hardware should be available in the library environment.

Greater ergonomic adaptation is coming. The entry of large flat-screen technology may mean that computers can be built into a larger variety of cases and furniture. People are experimenting with computers built into clothing, but it's hard to see exactly where that adaptation will go.

Hybridization of computers with various telephone, electronic book, geographic information systems, and other electronic devices has already resulted in a great deal of portability.

6 CHOOSING UTILITIES

Even with "Plug-and-Play" computers, not all the tools you need come with the computer. Before you turn on the first library computer, you need some utility software that will keep your computers healthy—such as virus checkers, backup programs, and a troubleshooting package. In addition, you may want some software that will make life easier for users and support staff. Other utilities might include disk recovery programs, screen savers, remote access software, security control, and system troubleshooting programs.

Virus protection software comes with some operating systems, but ends up being a separate purchase, simply because you must constantly update it to meet the challenge of new viruses. Other utilities represent bridges into technology that were not developed when operating systems or applications software were developed. Since early DOS versions, for example, the Windows operating system has begun to include a program to defragment the hard disk and another to compact the files on the hard disk.

TYPES OF UTILITIES

A host of utility programs have come and gone as each generation of new hardware and software developed. Very often when a utility was developed to meet an important need, it has subsequently been folded into either the hardware or the operating system. Windows 95, for instance, makes it unlikely that users will need memory management software or disk compaction software since those capabilities are provided by the operating system. The utilities that are needed to support a given generation of hardware and operating system are of two types:

- Utilities that would be required for any platform to make the system viable
- Utilities that are custom fit to make a platform more attractive but are not essential for it to function

UTILITIES TO MAKE THE PLATFORM VIABLE

DISK AND FILE RECOVERY

Programs like Norton Utilities supply a group of utilities that make it possible to handle files that go bad, disk drive recovery, disk drive analysis and tune-up, and tools for exploring your hard disk. Other software packages for file recovery, such as Recover NT, can be used with specific types of files and on particular operating systems. Utility programs will recover damaged files, but do not overlook the backup features built into most application software. Such features write the document you are working on to the disk every few minutes to insure that you do not lose a lot of work should the computer crash.

BACKUP

Programs to do systems-level backup have to match the hardware system used to store the data. It is usually easiest to purchase the software and hardware together. If it is not possible to purchase software and hardware as a package, select the software and hardware at the same time so that you can be sure the software has drivers for the backup hardware and that it will interface with your system.

Where it is necessary to perform some specific kind of backup, such as timed backup, network backup, or Web-server backup, it would be best to contact the software vendor to be sure the software you intend to purchase can perform the task. In the process, get suggestions about the best hardware to match to the software and the overall platform.

VIRUS PROTECTION

A few major vendors, McAfee, Norton, Cheyenne, and a few others dominate the market for virus protection software. Having virus protection is essential, but it is more complicated in some ways than other utilities. The software has to detect viruses on removable media drives, network file transfers, Internet downloads, and macro viruses in applications. Most vendors now have an automatic download system that updates workstation software periodically. Deciding how to set up the automatic update is an interesting question. Technicians may feel it simplest to download the updates and do the installation themselves. Network managers may handle the local installation with a login script or network management software. Users feel uncomfortable making decisions about viruses, so carrying out upgrades and occasional virus cleaning tasks may require a technician for the less confident users.

Virus protection software is not optional and is not a low priority.

It should be one of the highest priorities in making your computers operational. Suffering from viruses can immobilize the library for days and can be a labor intensive clean-up process.

MAINTENANCE MANAGEMENT

A variety of software fits under the rubric of maintenance, including software that tracks machine configuration remotely, troubleshooting programs, and housekeeping software. The library may encounter some of these programs when it relies on the parent organization for support. The parent organization may supply maintenance software and it will be up to the library to determine if there are any library uses to be made of the data collected by the system.

Overall, the purpose of maintenance management software is to use the central network and computer maintenance staff efficiently. To that end, the industry has convened the "Distributed Management Task Force" and tasked it with developing "Web-Based Enterprise Management" standards that will make it possible to centrally manage all the computing, network, and communications resources of the organization. Such software detects problems, notifies the IT department, then provides data for the IT department to contact the user, attempt remote fixes, troubleshoot further, and limit impact of a problem. Such software will access all types of devices, including desktop computers using software that is compliant with the Desktop Management Interface (DMI) standard and network devices that comply with the Simple Network Management Protocol (SNMP). Desktop and network software that can detect problems and audit system status. These programs use the Common Information Model (CIM) to organize, interpret, and present status to system managers.

Much of what can be accomplished with management software is intended to provide capabilities that optimize how maintenance is done. Where in the past users had to call technicians and attempt to explain a problem, now technicians can use sensing software to detect problems immediately, understand in perspective what users report, and provide rapid response to correct the exact system component or computer that is malfunctioning.

The packages that provide remote maintenance capability include commercial packages such as Bindview, IT Director, HP OpenView, Microsoft SMS, Novell ManageWise, and others. This category also includes a related type of software for auditing and metering software usage. Some of the auditing and metering software is provided or recommended by the Software and Information Industry Association (formerly Software Publishers Association). Most of these programs track hardware and software inventory, may allow remote installation and upgrade of software, and monitor licensing compliance. Such software packages, operating over a network, provide remote management by computer specialists. In this category, *PC Magazine* rated LANDesk Management Suite the best in its December 1, 1998, issue (*PC Magazine*, 1998). These software packages generally match the Desktop Management Interface (DMI) standard that defines remote management capabilities. This standard relies to some extent on software installed on the remote computer. Currently, Bindview EMS/Netinventory is very favorably reviewed according to *Computer Shopper* (*Computer Shopper*, 1999).

Other packages that manage the network should be capable of using the Simple Network Management Protocol (SNMP) to monitor network components, but may overlap with the desktop management software. Packages that monitor the network, such as LANDesk and OpenView, have added DMI capabilities.

On the desktop

Windows 98 includes an array of housekeeping functions, so housekeeping functions such as automatic cleanup of file caches, deletion of outdated files, and disk drive analysis have moved into the operating system. Users, with the advice of technical staff, can set operations to occur automatically when the computer is not in use.

On the horizon is new software that will have the ability to activate automatic repairs when necessary. Since chips are in many cases quite inexpensive, there may be a certain number of redundant components or areas of larger chips that activity can be rerouted through to avoid malfunctions. Already there are "hot fix" areas on disk drives that automatically bypass damaged areas, particularly in network servers. One self-repair software that bears watching is Motive Solo, which is currently going into consumer computers (Levin, 1999).

An organization may require a strategy for maintenance that goes beyond this discussion. Because problems can be remotely detected by software mounted on the network, planning is usually centrally controlled. In larger organizations, remote detection is put to use in order to minimize manpower costs and to make the most productive use of available specialists.

UTILITIES THAT IMPROVE THE PLATFORM BUT ARE NOT ESSENTIAL

SCREEN SAVERS

There are entirely adequate screen savers included with operating systems, such as Windows 98 and Windows NT. Screen savers can be inexpensively customized and are more likely to be of interest when used as "freebie" giveaways for advertising purposes. The one issue that must be addressed is whether to trust them as security devices. Windows has recently made the screensaver password more "pick-proof," so we may rely on it for first-level privacy protection. Users need the protection while their e-mail access is open and when they work on confidential documents.

FILE COMPRESSION AND ENCODING

Data that is transmitted from one location to another can be compressed—most usually using .zip type software—or encoded—most commonly using .uu encoding. Software is generally easy to locate and inexpensive to purchase, and most larger organizations put the software on the LAN so that it can be easily used by anyone who is logged on.

ADDITIONAL FONTS AND CLIP ART

Fonts provide the library with the ability to do brochures, posters, invitations, and flyers. Fonts come in two general types, Postscript and PCL, both of which generally allow text to be printed in a variety of sizes and treatments. Fonts, more correctly called typefaces, can be purchased or downloaded for free. Generally, worthwhile fonts are purchased to insure that the library has the legal right to use them. Collections of fonts, clip art, and stock photos are relatively inexpensive to purchase and can be used for routine newsletters and flyers. Choosing quality stock photos and clip art for publicity and high visibility Websites is more expensive. Several vendors offer these artistic resources in collections, either in retail stores or via the Web. Given the impact that illustration and text have, the use of well-designed materials will provide an aesthetic substance to be valued by patrons and donors.

DESKTOP IMPROVEMENT

Does your operating system come with an appointment monitoring software that has an address book function, calendaring, and the ability to track project tasks? Can you easily locate all the files for a project including the budget, Web files, and personnel documents? There are programs, usually integrated with e-mail or office applications software, that provide most of these functions. Whether they will benefit library staff is a judgement you may not have to make, since they are included with some other software. Some folks will use these utilities, others will not. Where possible, make them available for those who can use them profitably.

OTHER SOFTWARE

Communications software has not yet evolved to the point where Internet clients other than the Web browser are not needed, but we are fast approaching it. There is still some need for the traditional telnet and FTP clients to allow logon to remote computers and to allow file transfers.

Most libraries will purchase software for e-mail, security, and graphics editing.

E-mail will be more expensive to maintain than most software because it requires occasional management tasks such as setting up new users as well as troubleshooting. A key feature to look for is whether the e-mail program requires a separate server. For smaller libraries, shareware, such as Pegasus Mail, is available and is of excellent quality.

Security software, such as Ikiosk and Fortres, will do a good job of locking down the desktop. The first step in obtaining security software is to determine whether your users need mild or fairly stiff constraints. Look for a package that will deliver the level of security and flexibility that you feel is needed. Some of the features you may want to consider include remote administration, ability to lock Windows menus, ability to lock portions of applications, as well as compatibility with the network system you are using. Installing security software can be a complex task. Usually the best procedure is to install all the user software for a typically configured computer. Make a backup of that computer. Install the security software and adjust the settings to lock down those portions of the operating system and user software that users need. Use the system for a day or two to see how routine operations perform. If problems arise, it may be necessary to further adjust settings or allow applications software to have access to certain configuration files or work files.

Graphics software at its most primitive consists of paint/drawing software that comes with the operating system and with applications software suites. The graphics programs in these bundles have gotten better and offer some really useful capabilities, such as the Microsoft

Photo Editor which will make transparent .gifs and handle primitive textures. Other programs in suites such as Corel Photo Paint make adding special effects really easy. As an essential tool for occasional graphics, these programs are fine. Graphics artists will need Photoshop and special effects utilities to go with it. Web authors may require more sophisticated software as well.

Each utility purchased can be an expensive addition to your platform, because with the software comes the need to license it, upgrade it, train its users, and troubleshoot if it goofs up. Some strategies to minimize the impact of purchasing utility software seem in order.

Among the strategies to address utility software, one avenue is to find an economical way to site license the software for use by every member of the staff. This simplifies maintenance of the program and reduces the need to worry about which machines it might be installed on.

Another approach would be to purchase utilities for as few a number of users as possible, realizing that only the power users are going to be motivated to learn and use most utilities anyway.

Where specialized software is needed, such as with graphics, it may be optimum to have a specialized workstation set up. For graphics, the software can be set up on the same computer as a scanner, along with additional fonts and clip art libraries. If the computer is networked, users from several departments can use it and transfer completed artwork to the server where it can be accessed for inclusion in brochures, flyers, pathfinders, and other library materials. Digital cameras, which require their own software to download pictures, are a further reason for setting up a graphics workstation.

INTERNET UTILITIES

The biggest area of growth, especially of concern to libraries, is the area of browser utilities. Library patrons and staff members using the Internet and library databases need access to functioning, current versions of the following six types of Internet utility programs.

SOUND REPRODUCTION

If sound cards and speakers or headsets are available, the sound or multimedia software that comes with the operating system may suffice. Music libraries may require more sophisticated software and speakers.

TELNET, FTP, AND OTHER COMMUNICATIONS SOFTWARE

Telnet and FTP are included with Windows, but a more sophisticated version is usually needed to access some OPAC systems, administrative applications, and UNIX servers.

TEXT ACCESS SOFTWARE

Adobe Acrobat and a few other utilities provide access to documents the library may wish to store on the Web server for viewing and download. Library brochures, new books lists, newsletters, and other documents can readily be scanned in and made available to users from a Web page or via electronic reserve.

QUICKTIME, REALPLAYER, AND OTHER MULTIMEDIA ADD-INS

These programs make video recorded presentations available for a range of uses including children's storybook hours or "how-to" documents. Streaming audio plug-ins like RealPlayer can also make radio and TV programming available.

GENERAL PURPOSE APPLICATIONS SOFTWARE

Applications can be set to serve as a plug-in for your browser. When an Excel or Lotus spreadsheet is downloaded, the browser can be set to start the spreadsheet software. The spreadsheet starts and immediately loads the sheet that was downloaded by the browser.

PROGRAM INTERPRETERS

Java and XML are programs that operate small custom "applets" or programs that run on the computer the user is operating. Some screen handling functions, animation, or navigation tasks can then help the user through tasks without burdening the network with frequent data transmissions.

DEPLOYING UTILITY SOFTWARE

Proper deployment of utilities will make both staff and users capable of maximizing their work and reducing computer downtime.

Subjective considerations are often superimposed on what should be a management task, performed with a professional attitude. There should never be a discussion based upon notions such as whether either staff or patrons "deserve" to accomplish a certain function or use specific software. We have, unfortunately, begun to treat software as candy in many situations. Appropriate decisions do need to be made, and, clearly, consideration should be given to whether a given software is an advantage for individual productivity and organizational goal accomplishment. Within resources available, each person's ability to perform their duties and contribute to the growth of the organization should be maximized.

Typical software devoted to public access and to staff workstations are listed in Appendix F, "Software Deployment." This checklist is far from complete and will require updating as software changes. Most typically, utilities gradually over time become part of either the operating system or software suites.

IMPLICATIONS FOR LIFE CYCLE COSTING

Utility software quite often changes when the operating system that it goes with changes. When moving, for instance, from Windows 98 to Windows 2000, the version of Norton Utilities may have to be upgraded to match. The one type of utility software that may have a very different schedule is virus checkers. Ideally the person most responsible for support duties will maintain contact with vendor information to insure that new virus signatures and upgrades are installed on library computers as quickly as they occur, which may be monthly.

Costs for utilities can usually be managed with annual license fees and costed out of a miscellaneous supplies account. The greatest challenge is to provide for unforeseen circumstances. Ideally there should be a small budget, perhaps part of contingency funds, that will cover trial copies of new software.

When the first Web authoring software became available it was probably purchased as a utility and with no idea whether continuing support would be required. If an organization purchased Web software, it gave staff the chance to employ it creatively on behalf of the users. Today the Web is pervasive enough to consider a Web authoring editor as an applications program. In fact, it is so ubiquitous that two versions may be required. One version or type might be an authoring software for everyone in the organization and the second version or type should be a high-end Web authoring software that is very specialized, requiring a staff member who devotes considerable time to learning and using it.

Utilities can confound the budget process and frustrate the technical staff if they are not related to good management policies and actions. Users should be encouraged to minimize the impact of downloaded trial versions of software on operational equipment. It may be a good idea to have an older computer set aside for trial software downloads. Until you are certain that software is well-behaved, useful, and cost effective, it is wise to limit its potential for upsetting configurations. A good amount of judgement is also required. Software from experienced companies that is widely used may not pose a risk that shareware does. Poorly authored software may not integrate well with the primary applications such as word processors and Internet browsers that the library must rely on. Managers have a delicate balance to maintain between minimizing risk and facilitating library productivity.

7 CONFIGURATION MANAGEMENT

The moment you decide to upgrade, add new software, or consider changing the use for some of your computers, you will come face to face with the need to know which machine has what characteristics—the configuration. A computer's configuration consists of the particular software installed, the hardware parts, the accessories used with it, and the settings for all of the software and hardware.

It's not a big chore to make a record of the characteristics that make up a configuration, but it's one chore that is frequently overlooked when we're busy. If the library owns or operates within a networked environment, it is a task that becomes very necessary. It is also a task needed to keep track of the many special interfaces and options needed by library software, multimedia computers, and systems that are used for special functions. Possibly more important in the long run, configuration information is used in making budget decisions, management decisions, and sometimes in applying for grants.

RECORD KEEPING

Configuration management can be simple or complex. The simplest method is to use a form like that shown in Appendix G, which also tracks maintenance. Another form, in Appendix H, gathers information together in list form and could just as easily be kept in a spreadsheet. The most complex method is to adopt configuration management software that can keep track of computer hardware remotely and automatically, using the LAN. It would seem like a simple choice, perhaps driven by the question of how much time and resources we are able to devote to the record keeping process. Actually, the way we do configuration management may have more to do with our analysis of the effort we need to put into protecting ourselves from copyright infringement and from losses due to software and hardware malfunction.

Employees can load extra copies of applications software onto their machines or download software from the Internet. Because not everyone is careful about paying for downloaded software, the library can be exposed to the risk of using unlicensed software. Routine attention needs to be paid to tracking what software is installed to minimize the exposure to intervention by such organizations as the Software Publishers Association, which monitors and prosecutes copyright infringement. Networked programs for tracking installed software collect data every time a computer attached to the network is booted, so the process requires minimal effort to function.

Beyond copyright infringement, configuration management is a way to insure that computers can be restored to operation when catastrophic events such as disk crashes occur and when substantial upgrades are made. In either of these situations, detailed knowledge of the hardware, software, and peripheral devices installed on each machine is necessary.

Ideally, the documents that relate to the life cycle of each computer should be kept in a central location, probably the technician's office or central library files. The documentation that should be kept includes:

- A configuration information sheet
- The specification sheet that was used to order the equipment or the itemized invoice or packing slip that came with the computer at delivery
- The purchase order for the computer
- Original software disks and any backups that came with the computer or for software and hardware added at a later date
- Software license certificates
- Upgrade information showing where changes have been made from the original
- Connectivity information, including network addresses, machine login identities, and network protocols used

When the original software disks are kept with the documentation, there may need to be some minimum level of security for this file, probably a locked filing cabinet.

HARDWARE STANDARDS

Not all of the information in configuration management files is used routinely, but it is a reservoir for answering questions when a decision is made to add new systems or move equipment to new uses. It is very important to document some obvious things such as:

- Operating system version
- CPU type and model
- Type and amount of memory
- Type of hardware bus
- Peripheral ports
- Screen size and resolution
- Hard disk size, model, and interface type

- Peripheral drive speed and capacity
- Multimedia devices
- Network/modem devices

These notes will help in obvious situations such as finding a machine that has a USB port to set up a digital camera. The library management will need to know the type of equipment when budgeting for technology or when developing special projects.

Each of these annotations should also tell the kind of standard that the equipment and software meets if is not obvious. Not every standard can be documented, but the principal standards are often part of the nomenclature for the item. A network interface card, for instance, may be designated a "10/100" card, which tells you that it can be used in a 10 Megabits per second or a 100 Megabits per second network.

WORKFLOW

Where records are kept for routine use, some consideration of workflow is essential. Configuration files will have documents that originate in the purchasing process, are accessed by technicians, and may be referred to by whoever does routine maintenance and upgrades. It may be useful to start a configuration file even before equipment is delivered in order to safeguard the original specifications and the purchase documents. From there the next most likely record of equipment is probably going to be the physical inventory for the organization. Inventory numbers will be attached to everything that is considered equipment. Since the price of many computer accessories and peripherals has gotten cheaper, you may have to supplement the physical inventory with your own records to document less-expensive items. Scanners are a good example of computer equipment that costs less than $500 that may not be formally inventoried. The library may have to track such equipment through manual receipts or by maintaining an inventory in the OPAC where you can build item records for non-book items.

STANDARDS SOFTWARE

Public area machines in the library have security software, database access software, specific printer drivers, network addresses, and startup options that are needed to provide the services patrons expect. Communication between technical staff and library staff is essential in order to insure that machines remain in configuration.

When library staff open security to accommodate a patron, when machines have maintenance problems, when users "hack" a machine, or when someone saves a virus to the hard disk, staff need to readily return the machine to proper configuration. On evenings, weekends, or when technical staff are "maxed out" on other tasks, the problem can be diagnosed and handled by library staff. The key to being able to restore a machine to operation is to know the steps it will take to reinstall from a backup or to reinstall key pieces of software. Technical staff can document procedures as scripts that tell each step to perform. Larger libraries may have technical staff that are remote from the library and can respond to fix a machine either in person or from home via a network connection. Regardless of the way technicians are able to help, the library staff will have a role to play. They may assist in constructing scripts. With a script, a less knowledgeable staff member can "rescue" a machine, perhaps with some assistance from a staff member at home or a remote location. Library staff may also assist technicians by accurately reporting problems and assisting technicians in deciding whether a problem can be fixed remotely or if they need to come to the library to effect a repair.

Scripts for installing the public area machines are also very useful for libraries that have multiple locations. Using the same setup procedures can minimize downtime and keep a standard set of software installed. A script may be complicated and use a batch file or installer program to go through the process. The script can also be a written or typed list of the software and steps to go through. It all depends on how the staff is organized and who will be using the script.

As many of us learned in 1999, there is a lot of data that should be on hand to provide the basis for decision making about software upgrades. During the Y2K evaluation in each organization it was essential to know the "model" of software, the version, the most recent patch, and the manufacturer. If you are thinking "What is the model of a software?" it's simply that Microsoft, for example, produces Microsoft Office in a "standard" model, a "small business edition," and a "pro" edition. The version is the release number, as in WordPerfect 8, WordPerfect 9, or WordPerfect 2000—quite similar really to the production year for many types of equipment, including cars. A patch is a routine upgrade that fixes small problems between major versions. Patches may be called other things, for instance Microsoft terms them as "Service Releases."

LIBRARY CONFIGURATION

Most libraries have migrated to Windows clients and then to Internet access to provide database search service. In the process, they have installed software from vendors and modified the environment of their computers in ways that may be well beyond the routine configuration of other computers in the organization. There may have been a new version of Java added, the most current version of Adobe Acrobat added, specialized software for some news sites, or a proxy for the server. This type of software is not such a great problem for routine maintenance, particularly if good backups are available. The principal problem lies with configuring new machines where the configuration will have to be recreated from scratch. Organizational memory probably will not suffice. Records need to be kept, however brief, to insure that all the software on library computers that is used for access services can be identified when new hardware is installed.

WORKFLOW

Success in configuration management comes from having a procedure that is known, accessible, and easy. One way this can be accomplished is to store all the data on a shared network drive where everyone on staff can find it. When new equipment, upgrades, or repairs change the equipment the data can be updated. Of course it may be just as easy to keep a paper record. The hardest part of the management process is getting everyone to appreciate the time it takes to go to each machine to collect serial numbers, network IDs, or model numbers. If key people who work with the technology can agree to keep the data systematically and they work at collecting it as soon as events allow, the process will run smoothly.

Perhaps equally important in keeping configuration records is that most of the data be kept in the library. The library is accountable for equipment purchased on grants and in many cases the library decides quite independently when upgrades are needed. (It's not a good idea to wait until all the organization's administrative machines get upgraded or replaced to replace library computers. Database changes are likely to require you to upgrade a lot sooner than secretarial staff change computers.) Most computer centers and repair centers can be doing a great job but will be totally oblivious to user needs for configuration data.

END ITEM ACCOUNTABILITY

Responsibility for configuration does not stop with record keeping. During maintenance and troubleshooting, it is quite normal to swap major components such as monitors, disk drives, mice, printers, and so forth between machines. Some of these items are not inventoried, but they may affect configuration, particularly if drivers, cables, or system settings have to be changed to accommodate the swap. In such cases, updating records may suffice to account for unique situations. Those records should be the kind technical support people will look at so that they will know in the future if there is an unusual situation.

One question worth investigating is how much change must occur due to repairs or upgrade before you need to make a separate backup for a computer? If you have thirty machines and two of them have different parts or software, you have to keep at least two and probably three different software backups. Basically the question can only be answered in an individual setting. If a hard disk is changed to a different model from all the other computers, it may be easy enough to document the type of disk drive and the information from the BIOS about the number of tracks and sectors. With that information the system can be made operational after a failure or repair by using the software and configuration from another machine. If the computer is outfitted with a scanner and custom software for the scanner is installed, a separate software backup must be made or the installation disks for the software must be kept accountable and accessible. Ideally, a full backup should be made of that machine simply because if it has a problem and must be restored from scratch, it's a lot faster to restore from backup than it is to restore by reinstallation. A full backup also has the merit of protecting user-created files.

When items are permanently removed from a machine, such as a disk drive so that a larger one can be installed, tag the item carefully. Often spare parts that are in good condition get misplaced or mixed with repairable items, causing more expense and inconvenience. In larger organizations, ownership may be lost as well, unless some procedure for parts credits or quid pro quos has been established.

Overall, configuration management is an investment in the future, knowing that change will occur. It is a great way to double check the library's physical inventory and a time saver at many points in the equipment life cycle.

8 SETTING UP SHOP

Each library will have a somewhat different computing support picture, but the elements that go into computer support are fairly universal. There needs to be someone who can do each of the following tasks:

- Set up new computers and install software and utilities not installed by the factory
- Return unserviceable parts to the manufacturer for replacement under warranty
- Install application software and upgrade software including the operating system
- Make connections to the LAN, the Internet, and the library system
- Diagnose routine user problems such as computers freezing up, users losing files, disks not reading, etc.
- Troubleshoot equipment when it fails to function, such as the monitor not coming on or a mouse sticking
- Clean equipment and perform routine maintenance, such as replacing components
- Purchase repair parts and miscellaneous hardware
- Obtain tools and set up an area for hardware maintenance

A possibly important consideration to be made right from the beginning is whether technical support staff will have responsibility for audiovisual equipment. While a computer technician is not going to know how to troubleshoot and repair a slide projector, they can certainly rewire a bulb socket in an overhead projector or make up a coaxial cable connection for a television. Technicians who are hired for computer maintenance are not necessarily going to be prepared to deal with audiovisual problems, but many of the problems are going to be computer problems. Equipment such as data projectors are really computer peripherals, and other items such as video systems may contain computers. The library needs to advertise for the skills it will need. This may mean advertising for a computer technician who will do "minor audiovisual" work.

PATTERNS OF SUPPORT

Patterns of support are deeply influenced by the type of organization and the character of its leadership. Some patterns may be more hospitable to library operations than others. Let's look at the typical patterns and see where some of the strengths and weaknesses are in each of them.

The typical pattern where there is a library system with multiple library units is likely to have a weak local support team, occasionally consisting of library staff who have at least some technology experience, supported by a technically proficient central staff. This arrangement usually means that computer problems are done in batches and there may be delays in getting parts, technicians, and computers together. An advantage is that each site is supported in an identical fashion and problem solutions tend to get applied across the board.

Most often seen in larger academic libraries and corporations is the pattern where a technical staff is located in the library and there are other equally competent technical staffs located in other areas of campus. The downside of this arrangement is that relationships between technician groups can become part of institutional politics. An advantage is the focus of a group within the library on supporting very reliable access services.

Small organizations that are self-sufficient may be quite good at putting together competent service staffs. Most often, small libraries rely on parent organization technicians for support, but they will take on a few technical tasks to minimize service interruptions. The obvious downside to this is that self-sufficiency can become too great, causing technical support to rely too heavily on it. An advantage may be the ability to make changes quickly and use the newest technology since fewer people are involved in decision making.

One key point to make is that someone within the library staff needs to be knowledgeable about computers. That person may have to deal with security arrangements, computer set up, and user problems. Without a decent degree of computer literacy, the library will be at a daily disadvantage in dealing with technical issues.

PUTTING TOGETHER A SUPPORT ORGANIZATION

The hardware and software life cycles and life cycle costing come together in the operation of the support system. Daily decisions about the viability of individual computers feed right into the broader picture of what is cost effective. Criteria for determining how computers are maintained revolve around three criteria that are renowned for being the basis for tradeoffs: time, cost, and quality.

MAINTENANCE PHILOSOPHY

The tradeoff variables cost and quality tend to determine the maintenance philosophy that the organization employs and the quality of training that technical staff have or acquire. The maintenance philosophy and staff knowledge in turn go a long way to determining how quickly maintenance tasks are affected. Let's look in detail at the two steps of choosing a maintenance philosophy and finding appropriate staff training.

The first step in setting up a support organization is to have a maintenance philosophy. Whether out-sourced or in-house, four decisions will be made, if not by conscious decision, then by default:

1. Which systems are critical? This choice can help define which systems receive immediate attention, which systems' parts are purchased in advance, and which systems are maintained when funds are scarce.
2. How much down time can the library afford for the catalog or Web access? Support has to be prepared to have service restored within the time it takes to swap operations to a backup system. If the library cannot afford for these systems to be down at all, a "hot spare" that is already operating may be needed.
3. How will support be provided? This is related to cost. Are repairs to be done with original equipment parts from the manufacturer, locally available parts, or upgrade parts? The organization's purchasing philosophy will come into play here as well. If parts' sources are identified in advance, blanket order agreements can make it easy to obtain parts and to obtain a good selection.
4. When multiple computers are out of service at one time, are there clear guidelines as to how many parts may be cannibalized in order to get some percentage of the broken units back in service? Too lenient a policy may lead to machines being stripped beyond repair; too rigid a policy may limit the library's ability to meet user needs.

TECHNICAL STAFF TRAINING

The second step in setting a support plan is to establish some sources of training. Training of support staff is vital. There are two parts to training: basic skills training and awareness of the state of the art and technical trends. Due to the rapidity with which technology changes, most technicians need to improve basic skills frequently.

- Formal training prior to employment is ideal. Common certification programs include both generic and specialty certifications. The Computing Technology Industry Association offers A+ Certification, Novell, Microsoft, and Cisco, and other companies offer certification for their products.
- Certification is an ongoing need. In the next few years many systems will require someone with knowledge of Microsoft NT in the support group and that sort of knowledge can be obtained through certification training.
- Where the support organization has some depth or there is a regional library consortium, there may be a possibility of interning technicians in other organizations to gain experience with specific skills.
- Ideally, just as with professional staff, technicians should be involved in a mentoring relationship with more senior technicians or with peers who have varied skills. The time and effort it takes to obtain cross feed of skills may well save major costs that otherwise would go to offsite repair vendors.

Libraries have to rely on knowledgeable support staff to not only have basic skills but also to know whether new technology will integrate well with existing computers. Several methods exist for technical staff to keep up to date on changes in the state of the art:

- Trade shows provide specific information about software and equipment that only technical staff need have knowledge of. Major library conferences will exhibit new systems, and although not as detailed, may provide technical staff with some limited assistance.
- Exchanging visits to other libraries will help put technical matters in perspective with user needs and reinforce good technical housekeeping.
- Feedback from user groups can help support staff understand and respond to the needs as well as provide a means of understanding the best way to make technical decisions.

- Short courses provide hands-on instruction and important information on specific products.
- Newsgroups and vendor-sponsored technical forums often provide key information about products. An important consideration with sponsored information is of course whether it unduly influences upgrade decisions.

REPAIR METHODS

Computers are not amenable to a lot of local repair. Troubleshooting can help narrow down the difficulty, but parts are usually sent out for repair or the part is replaced. Replacing parts is not, however, a simple task. Repair technicians have to purchase the correct components, insure that they will fit the particular computer chassis, install software drivers, and adjust software to make sure that the new components work with existing components.

Probably the greatest challenge for local repair is the addition of accessories. Users often wish to keep up with new technology by adding devices that are new on the market. Newer devices require the addition of interface cards, drivers, and software. They may also challenge the power and speed of the older computer.

FACILITIES FOR TECHNICIANS

Where maintenance must be done away from the public area or office that a computer is normally operated in, technicians need a private workspace that is also convenient to use and relatively secure. Typical workspaces should include at least 120-square-feet per technician plus storage area. Counter or worktable space with convenient electrical outlets is needed for bench checking the computers. Lighting is a major concern since small parts are worked with. High-intensity desk lamps may be needed to augment standard fluorescent lighting.

TECHNICAL LIAISONS

Technical ability may make a major difference in the quality of support that is available. As much as the library may depend upon good reference librarians to work with patrons, it depends on knowledgeable technicians to contact and work with vendors. Technicians require long-distance telephone access, access to a fax machine, and Internet access.

USER SOFTWARE TOOLS AND MAINTENANCE ROLES

LIBRARY SELF SUPPORT

Wherever there are microcomputers and users there is a need for some group of "first aid" tools that supplement provisions for maintenance and user education that are formally provided by the organization. These tools are available when the support staff are too busy, or the task too minor to warrant changing work priorities. There are usually a few knowledgeable users who can handle the routine tasks safely.

Tasks

To keep resources aligned within reasonable boundaries, it's important to set a standard in terms of time and expectations for computer support accomplished within the work group. Somewhere around two hours of effort you reach a point where the amateur "chip hound" should consider holding further work for support staff. Certain tasks should also be reserved, in most cases, for support staff. One of these is changing LAN drivers. The setup procedures can change frequently enough that the workgroup "guru" needs to at least sit through a fresh installation of drivers about every three or four months or consider that they are rusty enough to forego doing troubleshooting. Remember too, that a really important service that the workgroup guru can put their talents into is observing the symptoms of each problem, documenting them, and ruling out common user goof-ups before the support staff specialists are called.

Within the work group, some useful and potentially vital tasks are well within the realm of most in house gurus. These include:

- Memory Management: As applications are added, there are often small memory resident programs that are loaded to facilitate operations. A good example is Microsoft Office, which loads a small memory-resident program to facilitate calling all of the Microsoft applications. Someone needs to be aware of the possibility that too many of these small programs can accumulate and bog down the computer. Given that modern operating systems are very good at memory management, the primary focus for users is to detect the need for more memory units to be added to the computer.
- Virus Prevention: Not only does virus detection software have to be loaded onto each computer, but occasionally viruses are

detected and one disk or another needs to be "cleaned" to get rid of a virus. In addition, the virus program requires occasional upgrading. Response to virus detection must be rapid, because users are unable to work until the situation is remedied.

- Disk Compaction: As files are added and deleted, a hard disk will develop spaces which once were occupied by a file, but have been left over after a newer file was placed on the disk. Someone needs to run a utility that will move all of the files so they are contiguous with the others and the empty space is consolidated for use by new files.
- Ordering Repair Parts: Memory upgrades, printers, and replacement components can all be ordered by someone who understands computer specifications within the organization or is willing to learn. Purchases will usually be made to extend the lifetime of computers that cannot be immediately replaced, but not to continue outdated equipment where its use is likely to limit workgroup productivity. Ergonomic parts and accessory software may also be usefully purchased by a knowledgeable user.
- Liaison with Support Staff: Scheduling and assistance with completing upgrade projects often requires someone who understands how users function. The user who can balance between the priorities both users and support staff have will be able to help both groups.
- Troubleshooting: Determining what is wrong with a computer is an important first task that can be accomplished by rebooting, switching major components, checking cables, interpreting system behavior, resetting system parameters, and insuring software is properly installed.

Each of these tasks can reach a point where they compete with a "guru's" normal work. Members of the work group should be led to expect occasions when the guru deflects pleas for assistance in order to get their own work completed.

Support for User Training Needs

Training support within the work group addresses one of the most expensive elements connected with microcomputers. To effectively learn enough of any application software that you can utilize its flexibility requires a great investment in time. Whether through formal training or through self-training, a lot of time goes into trying commands and learning the limitations of the software. I can readily imagine a minimum of 50 to 60 hours of use as the minimum to become proficient in most word-processing software. A spreadsheet may be the easiest to master, while a database program could literally take months to fully appreciate.

Two factors contribute to effective training to use software: the need to accomplish a task and the interest in learning something new. Most often, library staff will attend training or use a packaged training program when they approach a new task for the first time and learn that they need specific software to accomplish the task. Effective training, therefore, needs to be very responsive to project needs, the needs of new employees, and training when upgrades occur.

User toolkit

Knowledgeable users should have access to a small toolkit that may cost $20 in the local computer store or office supply. It should contain nut drivers, tweezers, screwdrivers, a parts tube, and a grasping tool for retrieving items from tight spaces. It should be augmented by a small, bright flashlight, a mirror on a telescoping handle, a keyboard vacuum cleaner, and a small pocketknife. These tools should more than accommodate retrieving bits of broken floppy disks, changing out an occasional interface card, moving cables, and completing network setups. Some plastic ties, canned air for dusting, and parts tags should finish the kit.

These tools should augment the basic library toolkit, which staff can depend on to have an electric drill, drill bits, common pliers, needle-nose pliers, a hammer, extension cord, large flashlight, straight-blade and Phillips-head screwdrivers, a crescent wrench, vise-grips, wire cutters, staple gun, glue gun, tape measure, and level.

SUPPORT BY TECHNICAL STAFF

COMMUNICATIONS

Technical staff may be useless unless they can be communicated with. When the library needs assistance in meeting an equipment or communications problem, the staff must be able to reach the technicians. When the technical staff are troubleshooting equipment, they need to be able to readily reach vendor help desks, parts suppliers, each other, and consortium technical staffs. Such communications are best enhanced by providing a cell phone. In smaller libraries, a beeper may be all that fits the budget, but a high-quality wireless telephone should be made available for the technician to use when working on computers that may be some distance from a telephone.

Technical staff also need to communicate with equipment they maintain. When servers are set up, they should be equipped with paging software so that when a server encounters problems an automatic monitoring routine can trigger a call to the pager or cell phone of the duty technician.

STOCKING UP—SUPPLIES

Among the supplies that should be on hand to keep computers operating, there are some inexpensive but very necessary items. First and foremost among them are some replacement mice or trackballs and some keyboards. It may be that computers are purchased with replacement parts guaranteed, so the library need only stock up on a couple of cheap ($10–$25) keyboards and two or three cheap ($5) mice that will keep things running until the manufacturer can send replacements.

Repairs often necessitate moving data off hard drives temporarily. This can be a big job if a hard drive is replaced or a small job if there is a backup and you just have to reboot and restore. For whatever eventuality, it is a wise idea to have a few floppy disks as well as Zip disks and/or writeable CD-ROM disks if there are computers equipped for them. The Zip disks and CDs can be used to move a basic computer configuration and user files.

Other commonly needed supplies include BIOS batteries, parallel cables to connect printers, SVGA cables for monitors and projectors, "drop" cables that run from the network interface card in the computer to the network wall outlet, cleaning disks for disk drives, screen cleaner and wipes, spare power strips, flashlight batteries, parts tags and pens, and spare cables for connecting disk drives and for connecting CD-ROM drives to the interface cards inside the computer.

Security items, particularly security cables and locking drive covers, are needed when new computers arrive. A backup supply of each of these items would be good to cover unforeseen circumstances.

At some point the library may wish to have a supply of ergonomic accessories such as palm rests, copy holders, adjustable-height keyboard trays, and glare shields. Many of these items have become common in office supply sources, so there may not be a need to keep them on hand unless it is necessary to purchase in volume.

TECHNICIAN'S TOOLS

In Appendix I is a list of tools that will probably be essential for technicians to use in routine maintenance. Invariably as multimedia accessories such as audio discs and digital projectors enter the library inventory, the need for a supply of spare cables and unusual connectors and adapters will arise. Technicians need a bench stock budget to have these items on hand.

As much as technicians need hardware tools, they also need software tools and publications. Typical technical books tend to be in the $50 range and so a budget of at least $300 per year would seem a reasonable minimum. Clearly there is a tradeoff between technicians' initial knowledge base and the number of technical books they may require.

9 SUPPORT

SUPPORT PROCEDURES: WHO DOES IT?

Technical support to keep microcomputers and other technology operating will usually come from the parent agency or from a vendor. The library is most likely to maintain a technical staff only when it is large or when it also operates its own integrated online library system. Qualified technicians should perform the really technical tasks.

Technicians can handle the tougher technical tasks, but there are plenty of technical duties in the library that ought to be performed by knowledgeable library staff. Some of these duties will include:

- Placing new CD-ROMs into dedicated workstation drives
- Unpacking and placing new equipment
- Doing initial troubleshooting to provide an idea of the urgency of a problem and to see if a simple fix like running a virus scan will cure the problem
- Assisting other users with routine problems
- Staff training in software and computer literacy
- Moving equipment safely to new locations
- Contacting repair facilities and preparing equipment to be shipped
- Locking and unlocking security to accommodate special situations

The extended technical support required to keep computers operating will have to come from a knowledgeable technician. There are several considerations about the quality of support and the way it functions, but the initial concern will be how that support activity is paid for and how that cost will impact the life cycle cost of the technology.

To properly connect support costs with the life cycle budget, you first must know the basis upon which support costs are predicated. Some possible formulations for support costs include:

EXTENDED WARRANTY

Extended warranty is where the vendor that sold the equipment provides parts and repair for an additional fee. Like any extended warranty, you usually purchase a service such as insurance and make sure that "original equipment" parts are used for repair. Since there is a lesser likelihood that computer equipment will break in the initial few years of the life cycle, this is a good source of revenue for the vendor.

Over the years, warranties have changed in nature. In 1980 it was a real benefit to have a maintenance contract with a local vendor. Computers were new and local dealers could provide training and extended handholding. Repairs were expensive and manufacturers' repair shops were often overburdened with work. Gradually, third-party contractors developed, and at a large corporate level became the maintenance vendors of choice for some organizations. Computer makers themselves are better providers of service today, having honed their support organizations to supply call center contact for routine problems, parts for upgrade and maintenance, and extended warranties for reasonable prices.

Today, maintenance is relatively expensive in the local area. This is because the local maintenance shop has to find compatible parts, often from the manufacturer, and weed through user questions to really find out the true nature of maintenance problems.

The biggest exception to the vendors for repairs is when the computers are "clones" and are only sold through a local dealer. There is usually a simplicity in relying on that local dealer for repairs if they have the reputation and ongoing willingness to do good maintenance. In lieu of a local dealer, library technicians can maintain clones with commercially available parts, since there is less of a performance benefit to maintaining uniformity—clones are less likely to meet top of the line *PC Magazine* benchmarks.

INVESTMENT COST PAID TO THE PARENT AGENCY REPAIR SHOP

Some parent agencies require that a flat percentage of the purchase cost be paid to them in order to provide service. Since this is an internal transfer, the process is relatively simple. Payment may be a one-time fee or there may be annual charges.

ORGANIZATIONAL CONTRACT

Some support agencies may charge the organization as a whole. This cost may or may not be parceled out to the work center level. It is best to find out what the pro-rata share is for the library, because support costs can be shifted without warning and it is best to have good information available.

"ON-CONDITION" COST

The cost of repairing equipment when its condition changes. This is the most difficult to deal with financially because, if there is no up-front cost charged, you need to estimate the annual repair cost and have that amount programmed into the budget. To arrive at a cost, find out how frequently computers go into the shop. If no organizational data is available, estimate once every three years. Now estimate the average annual cost.

Here is a sample way of guessing a reasonable support cost if you have no historic data, but do have some computers already in use. Use 3 percent of the purchase cost, multiplied by the number of computers, to estimate repair costs for the year. An example may help:

TABLE 1—ESTIMATING SUPPORT COSTS

Purchase cost of computer	$2,100.00
3 percent of cost	$63.00
Number of computers	X 32
Total cost per year	$2,016.00

This is a very crude way to estimate the cost. If you have a good first-year warranty, the library may only have to pay shipping costs for returned parts and computers. This simple example also illustrates the possibility that it may be cheaper to replace machines than to maintain them. Other costs such as shop fees for troubleshooting could make maintenance much more expensive.

PLANNING

To properly choose a maintenance program that is the most economical for the library requires comparing the cost of principal tasks fairly between the different sources of support. A matrix that is something like the following may be helpful:

TABLE 2—COMPUTER MAINTENANCE OPTIONS

COST INPUTS	in-house	local vendor	manufacturer
user assistance			
troubleshooting			
parts replacement			
configuration for new databases and uses			
upgrade			

Use this matrix to analyze the cost of staff time, replacement parts, and peripheral costs such as shipping, restocking fees, and shop fees.

TASKS PERFORMED BY TECHNICAL STAFF

Some tasks may be performed by either library staff or technical staff, including such things as:

- Preventative maintenance cleaning of disk drives, keyboards, and screens
- Installation of browsers, browser plug-ins, and adaptation of browser configuration
- Installation and configuration of security software and virus checkers

Generally, it would be better to have technicians help with:

- Installing any network hardware or software
- Configuring telecommunications software
- Replacing hardware components inside the computer case
- Installing software that requires password or electronic keys to activate
- Installing security and virus detection software
- Installing database software for Web-based access

THE SUPPORT ENVIRONMENT

HELP USERS BUILD A SUPPORTIVE ENVIRONMENT

Users, particularly the library staff, can often be the key to successful computing because their behavior can determine how well software and hardware work. Ideally, every user should know enough about computing to manage files so that their use is facilitated and no damage occurs to software. The golden rule of file management, as in much of library work, is to store things in such a manner that they can easily be located and retrieved. That means making subdirectories on hard drives and network drives for projects, routine collections of graphics, letters to vendors, and other routine collections of documents. Using subdirectories also insures that users do not accidentally delete system programs when they erase other files. Important files should be stored on a network drive. A network drive is easier and more necessary to backup than a user workstation and insures that files will not be destroyed by a local hard-drive crash. It would be good to emphasize to staff that files and programs should not be placed in the root directory on a workstation, and never should they erase what is in the root directory. As a last resort, install security software to insure that less well-trained staff do not have access to critical parts of the operating system or the hard disk.

USER SELF-SUPPORT

It is more convenient than ever for users to help themselves. Manufacturers of software and hardware have increasingly developed self-help sites to minimize the cost of supporting customers after the sale. Most such services operate over the Web, making access very convenient. The key to such services is having a member of the library staff that is confident enough, knowledgeable of terminology, and able to use basic tools to carry out basic troubleshooting tasks. In smaller libraries such troubleshooting can go a long way to having equipment in operation well before a technician can be dispatched. It also is a good way to help contain costs.

To implement a self-support program, the library should probably compose a Web page or set of saved Web links that list the major sites which can be helpful. Start with the support page of the equipment manufacturers for the computers, software, and accessories owned by the library. Then consider sites such as *www.zdnet.com* and others that have helpful tips on the Web. Many such sites provide broad spectrum troubleshooting tips for very specific problems. Finally, consider for-profit sites that charge on a per-access basis for troubleshooting.

RESPONSE TIME

Support staff need to communicate back to users fairly quickly after a request for assistance is made. The toughest part about responding is insuring that all requests are tended to within a reasonable amount of time. A useful way to do this is to have one person assigned the task of follow-up to insure that users that have to wait at least get a message that support requests are backed up.

USER FEEDBACK

Feedback is a two-way street. Support staff need to listen and evaluate comments made about their performance. Users also need feedback when their expectations are unreasonable. Discourage technicians from making fun of users (at least within range of their hearing).

DOCUMENTING USER REQUESTS

However good you become at support, there are occasional dustups. You can minimize problems with users by documenting every user request. Most organizations only accept requests by e-mail, even if the user walks into the support office. This insures that the request is received in a manner that it can be documented and provides the opportunity to get enough detailed information to address the problem. Also, users sometimes realize the correct solution to their problem just through the thought process necessary to formulate the request.

Ideally, a work order number ought to be assigned to user requests. That signals to the users that you are taking the request seriously, it establishes a sequence for fulfilling requests, and implies that you are logging the requests (you are, aren't you?).

HOT SPARES AND WIPEOUT SYSTEMS

Networks, Web servers, library system servers, and communications servers are fairly crucial resources that we cannot do without. Today, realistically, when half our journal collections reside on distant database systems in full text, we need our network systems up and running. Several ingredients go into accomplishing the task of having our systems operating 99 percent of the time. One is to have a spare computer that matches our server on standby, or a "hot spare." Another ingredient is to have redundant equipment, particularly disk drives and memory, so that equipment failure is easily remedied.

PREVENTATIVE MAINTENANCE

Annually, it is wise to see that all equipment is surveyed and minor preventative maintenance attended to.

PHYSICAL CLEANING

This should include cleaning the floppy drives, cleaning the mouse, blowing dust out of the case, and checking cables for frays and connections.

ELECTRONIC HOUSEKEEPING

For staff machines, this may simply mean checking that sufficient disk space remains for daily activities. For public area machines, where automatic housekeeping routines in the operating system may be turned off to accommodate security software, there may be more that needs to be done. The hard drive should be checked for bad sectors, the caches emptied, and junk files cleaned off the desktop. Power supply cables need to be checked to be sure they are clear of debris and that wires are safely arranged.

BUILDING NEW PRODUCT EXPERTISE

Everyone in the organization probably has a role in keeping up with new technology. There are newsgroups that help provide information, magazine Websites, databases, print subscription magazines, and trade shows. People will best be able to monitor products they have a vested interest in, so reference staff will have a motivation to keep up on local database software, technical staff should keep up on systems and networks, and library technical services staff will probably be most interested in library system functions. Some interests, such as Web authoring and word processing, will be of interest to everyone.

Trying out new software and finding the right combination of tools is an ongoing process that needs some managing. The key to making good decisions is validation. If the new product is well reviewed, used profitably by another organization, and is compatible with computers and networks in your organization, then it is a candidate for adoption. A routine discussion with the most technically literate staff members is a good way to make purchase decisions.

PERFORMANCE MONITORING

Computer maintenance problems tend to be aggravating enough to get immediate attention. Monitoring the performance of the computers used by the library is a bigger and subtler problem than that. There are two principal ways to monitor equipment. One way is manually, using repair records and annual check ups. Another way is through constant automatic monitoring. Either method has the aim of knowing what components are likely to wear out, whether maintenance costs are rising on a given group of machines, and whether productivity is hampered by poor machine performance.

However performance is considered and monitored, some basics that need to be done include:

- Assign each machine an identity number or mnemonic
- Document the configuration of each machine
- Document maintenance problems
- Track vendor maintenance releases and their implementation within the library

GROWING THE SUPPORT ORGANIZATION

If the support for library computing is to keep up with changes in vendor software, install maintenance upgrades, and keep the organization at or near the state of the art, some resources are needed to nurture the support element. Some of the basics include:

- Support staff should be included in annual library system update meetings held by vendors
- Technicians should be encouraged to go to regional trade shows and national meetings when they occur in the local area
- Professional training and certification should be encouraged
- A budget for technical materials should provide repair manuals

LIBRARY REALITY

Priorities in a library or information center have to place public service first. The machines that get the best response time and most complete attention should be those used by the public. For support staff unaccustomed to supporting external customers, that may come as a major surprise. Every organization has some basic priorities of course. Network servers get special attention because without them all the other computers are dead in the water. The executive officer, when that person is preparing an annual budget, may get a temporarily high priority. The business manager does not, however, get a routinely higher priority; neither do staff computers. Transaction computers at service desks probably deserve second-highest priority.

CONNECTING MAINTENANCE TO LIFE CYCLE COSTING AND DECISION MAKING

MISSION SENSITIVITY OF RESOURCES

Since support activities are related to the lifeblood of modern electronic librarianship, there is a real tendency to let support become the driving force in decision making. Support team members may value their convenience more highly than service to patrons. Librarians have a continuing need to relate the impact that support issues have on patrons so that the support staff are always aware of the environmental impact of their work. Managers may find some method of monitoring the projects and tasks handled by technicians and the priorities set by library staff as key elements in understanding whether support staff are properly employed. Managers should, of course, be actively keeping technical staff up-to-date on changing priorities and needs from the library perspective.

SUBSTITUTION AND BACKUP

Across the computers in the library are a range of computers that incorporate a variety of performance levels, usually purchased at different times. It may be crucial to know where machines can be moved from less critical locations to replace key staff and public access computers that are down for maintenance. While good configuration management can resolve immediate problems of selecting which machine to move, good planning can assure that a machine is available. For really crucial machines, such as servers and circulation computers, it may be important to have backups of critical computers that have been checked in advance for compatibility to insure that a transfer of function can take place with minimum dislocation.

WORKLOAD SHIFTING

Where it is difficult to adequately provide a backup within library resources, it may be possible to share in a pool of backup equipment, such as servers, within the larger organization. Investigate the possibility that such a pool is available and secure advance agreement to make taking advantage of the pool possible on short notice.

10 SUMMARY OF THE PROCESS

Having analyzed the library's needs, assessed the organization's finances for continued support, and matched finances to equipment purchases and level of support, there should be a coherent plan that provides the foundation for continued decision making.

We can build a brief example of a plan for a small public library where there are to be about 30 public area computers. There is a need to do staff training and train users in the Internet. Without getting into the cost of the library system server and software, the costs might begin to look like the data given in the table on the next page.

This rough outline of costs should help start your thinking. It does not contain costs for a library software system and it does not document the assumptions that are made about the environment in which it would be applied. There are no costs projected for maintenance, repair, replacement, and new technology. There are some assumptions made that are fairly obvious:

- Some items are maintained "on condition," in other words only when they break
- The network operating system is not under maintenance, which for software would mean that any upgrade is a new purchase

Other budget and planning areas need some work and there are a number of questions that need answers:

- Support is assumed, but has the library decided how to handle the overall support needs, including training?
- When the three years of maintenance that come with the computers runs out, will one technician be sufficient to keep all the computers operating?
- Will the technician train to new levels of certification/knowledge to keep up with new system demands and to become the supervisor if another technician is hired?
- Are any support and networking needs provided through the parent institution?
- Will the technician be capable of handling the tasks for setting up database access or will it be necessary to hire a Webmaster?
- How will replacement cost be allocated? Is there a fund where a set aside amount can be retained across fiscal year boundaries or will there have to be a special allocation at a future date?

SUMMARY TABLES

TECHNOLOGY PLAN — 1ST YEAR

Item	Purpose	Purchase Cost	Maintenance Cost	Consumable Cost	Total Cost
Microcomputers w/Windows	Public area terminals, training	2,100×32=67,200	3 yrs included		67,200
Printers	Public printer, staff printer	3,200	on condition	500	3,700
Network software	Network operating system	4,500			4,500
Network server	PC with SCSI drives	4,500	3 yrs included		4,500
Web server	PC with SCSI drives	4,500	3 yrs included		4,500
Data projector	Training, public programs	5,000	on condition		5,000
Network hub	Connect PCs to Internet interface	800	on condition		800
Internet interface & install	Telecom set up	2,600	on condition		2,600
Building wiring	Network	7,500			7,750
Software for 4 public PCs	Word processor, spreadsheet	1,200		250	1,200
PC Support books	Minimum for support staff	300			300
Support tools	Recommended tools	350			350
Staff computers (5)	Circulation, reference, processing	2,100×5=10,500			10,500
Software for staff computers	Desktop suite	1,600			1,600
Troubleshooting software	Norton utilities, other	600			600
Security software	Site license	500			500
Utility software	Virus checker	500			500
Support staff of one	Maintain all computers	28,000			28,000
Repairs	Maintain all computers	2,100			2,100
Total:					146,200

TECHNOLOGY PLAN — 2ND THROUGH 4TH YEARS

Item	Purpose	Purchase Cost	Maintenance Cost	Consumable Cost	Total Cost
Support staff of one	Maintain all computers		28,000/yr		28,000
Repairs	Maintain all computers		2100/yr		2,100
Upgrade staff software	3rd year upgrade		1000/3rd yr		333
Upgrade virus checker	For all computers		450/yr		150
Printer paper & toner	Public & staff use			500	500
Minor supplies	Repairs			200	200
Total per year (for 3 years):					31,283

Libraries starting to acquire large numbers of computers and Internet access for the first time will have decisions to make that can only come from knowing the institutional environment well. The initial focus on obtaining and installing equipment must be done with full realization that networking and providing the services that go with Internet access take staff time and devotion. Fully investigating the cost of support staffing to find the right balance between self-support, a library technical staff, and consortial or parent organization support is crucial in providing the level of access that today's users expect.

REFERENCES

REFERENCES

Avery, Susan. 1999. "'Uptime' is a Mark of a Quality PC Supplier." *Purchasing Magazine* January 14.

Computer Shopper. 1999. "Bindview EMS/Netinventory." May 13.

Corbly, James E. 1997. "Upgrading Application Software: Problems and Perspectives." *Information Technology and Libraries* 16, No. 4: 193–196.

Dean, Edwin B. 1996. "Design for Cost." Found at *http://mijuno.larc.nasa.gov/dfc/dfcst.html*. Originated May, 5, 1994, revised May 5, 1996.

Hardin, Joseph, and John Ziebarth. 1998. *Digital Technology and its Impact on Education*. Urbana-Champaign, IL: National Center for SuperComputing Applications. Available at *www.ed.gov/Technology/Futures/hardin.html*, text under "Assumptions, accessed December 1999.

Kinnaman, Daniel E. 1995. "The Leadership Role: Budgeting for Technology." *Technology & Learning* 15, No. 5 (February): 70.

Levin, Carol. 1999. "Self-Service Repairs." *PC Magazine* August 10.

Oberlin, John L. 1994. "Departmental Budgeting for Information Technology: A Life-Cycle Approach." *Cause/Effect* (Summer).

PC Magazine. 1998. "PC Labs Reviews: Taming the PC Jungle." December 1.

Perkins, Matthew. 1998. "Assessing Computer Upgrades." *Women in Business* 50, No. 3 (May): 50.

Young, Jeffrey R. 1998. "Microsoft Tries to Answer Campus Critics with a New Pricing Plan for its Software." *Chronicle of Higher Education* 45, No. 2 (September 4): A40.

APPENDIX A: ASSESSING THE ORGANIZATION

This first Appendix provides a checklist to begin assessing the organizational environment. Although managers should routinely be aware of the environment in which budgets are developed, a check to make sure that there are no blind spots is useful. This is not an all-encompassing checklist and does not go further afield into judgment areas such as whether the organization is growing, retrenching, or in a steady state with respect to revenue and profit. Some organizations may foster technological innovation more than others. Look at the organization as an outsider would, and if you can manage it, have a professional colleague do the looking by asking you probing questions about the way budgets are handled.

- Analyze budget procedures to know when, where, and how major budget items are built into the budget cycle.
- Identify cost category definitions within the budget.
- Know the historical budget for the library in technology related areas.
- Prepare an estimate of cost for the life cycle of the library computers and software.
- Fit the annual costs to the best locations in the budget.
- Estimate costs that will not fit the budget or the budget categories.
- Find creative financial resources to cover any difference between estimated life cycle cost and the amount budgeted.

The process of life cycle costing begins with developing knowledge of the budget process within your organization. You will want to know about the following:

- The starting and ending dates of the budget year.
- If a justification process precedes the publication of the budget, i.e., is the budget changeable?
- What process is used to preload dollar amounts into each budget category, i.e., does it come from previous year amounts, are there percentages automatically allocated, or do work centers have the opportunity to request amounts?
- Who has the authority to alter pre-loaded amounts?

- Which categories can funds be switched between and who has the authority to transfer funds between categories?
- What funds are already earmarked or encumbered for some purpose? (For example, money in the budget may be targeted to pay the phone bill and you have to be sure not to spend it on something else.)
- What sources of revenue funds accrue to library accounts? Does this include non-appropriated funds?

APPENDIX B:
LIFE CYCLE COSTING

Customize this checklist in a spreadsheet to list all the hardware and software needed to fully implement the technology project. The *supplies* and *upgrade* costs have been listed here as columns in order to focus consideration of costs on the line items. Clearly some items may not fit easily into a category. Telecommunications costs, network wiring, and some of the support staff facilities need to be separate line items. As suggested in Chapter 10, staffing and training—whether from inside or outside the organization—need to be line items as well.

You can download this form from this book's Website, *www.smu. edu/~nhowden/micros.html.*

LIFE CYCLE COSTING

	initial cost	upgrade	supplies	cost to replace	cost to maintain	total
Cost of equipment						
desktop computers						
printers						
projectors						
scanners						
bar code readers						
Cost of software						
word processor						
spreadsheet						
database						
graphics						
clip art						
virus detection						
bibliography program						
fonts						
security program						

APPENDIX C: NEEDS ASSESSMENT

Needs assessment is complex and should encompass information from both staff and managers. Reaching goals requires a combination of choosing reasonable objectives and using tools and procedures effectively. This form is formatted to suggest that documenting needs is best done in an abbreviated narrative format. Individual or group brainstorming would be good sources for data. Technicians who will advise on selecting software and hardware need documented information about needs to fully understand not only the need, but something about what range of solutions will actually work. It would be ideal to invite a technician to sit in on the brainstorming.

You can download this form from this book's Website, *www.smu.edu/~nhowden/micros.html*

NEEDS ASSESSMENT

Office: _____   Date: _____

Task/Work area:	Ability needed or problem that must be solved:	Suggested software/hardware:	Impact/Benefit of improved technology:

Work Center manager: _____
                                 signature

APPENDIX D: TECHNOLOGY PLAN

Technology plans are complex and multi-faceted. Good managers ensure that each element of a plan is related to library goals and objectives.

The strategy for upgrading and replacing computers and software should be fully documented. Repair and training schemes should also be documented. Most important to actually making the process work is connecting the costs to the objectives that are being met. This form would be best set up in a spreadsheet where the "Purpose" field can be sorted. Whether you use a purpose, an objective, a department name, or a project name, you will probably want to sort all the information by purpose, by category (software, hardware, communications) or by some field not shown on the form, such as type of maintenance support.

Having this data collected in an easy to manipulate format in a spreadsheet will facilitate manipulating the costs and the budget to get them to match. To facilitate this manipulation, you can download this form from this book's Website, *www.smu.edu/~nhowden/micros.html.*

TECHNOLOGY PLAN

Item	Purpose	Purchase Cost	Maintenance Cost	Consumable Cost	Total Cost

APPENDIX E: SOFTWARE USAGE AGREEMENT

You may shudder at the notion of asking an employee to sign an agreement like this. My intent in supplying it is simply to reach a level of honesty and clarity that is sometimes lost in organizational communications. It may be that you can accomplish the same end verbally or by placing the content in a memo. Remember too that the organization has obligations to treat each employee fairly, to communicate with employees, and to foster staff development.

You can download this agreement from this book's Website, *www.smu.edu/~nhowden/micros.html.*

SOFTWARE USAGE AGREEMENT

Software Name:	
Version:	
User Name:	
Date:	

As the user of the above listed software, I hereby agree to the following terms for using this software in my daily duties:

1. The library will not provide training classes in this software. Access to computer-based tutorials, manuals, or training paid for by the library will be at the sole discretion of the library management.

2. Technical staff will not troubleshoot performance problems with software. Technical staff will be limited to installing and removing the software from the computer.

3. The user of this software will not proselytize the use of this software with other library employees.

4. Users of this software are encouraged to share insights in its use with other authorized users of the same software within the organization.

5. The user of this software is responsible for insuring that documents produced from it are appropriately formatted to be compatible with software supported by the organization or in a readily transferable format such as rich-text format (.rtf), document interchange format (.dif), or plain text.

_____
Signed

_____
Date

APPENDIX F: SOFTWARE DEPLOYMENT CHECKLIST

Looking at software from the users' perspective is important to good morale and organizational effectiveness. This form, with local modifications, can be used to see the software needed to provide all the functionality for staff and patron access.

The form can be downloaded from this book's Website, *www.smu. edu/~nhowden/micros.html*.

SOFTWARE DEPLOYMENT CHECKLIST

PATRON ACCESS		
Software	*Brand*	*Version*
Adobe Acrobat		
QuickTime		
anti-virus		
sound		
.zip file decompression		
.uu file decoding		
security		
telnet		
RealPlayer		
SOFTWARE FOR STAFF		
Adobe Acrobat		
QuickTime		
anti-virus		
sound		
.zip file decompression		
.uu file decoding		
forms management		
bar code maker		
telnet		
FTP		
mail		
additional fonts		

APPENDIX G: MICROCOMPUTER CONFIGURAION

Configuration records and maintenance records should be kept in the same location since they need to be consulted together and updated simultaneously as actions are taken. Maintenance records should have enough configuration information to identify individual machines. Both forms will be needed to discuss detailed maintenance problems with offsite repair agencies and vendors.

MICROCOMPUTER CONFIGURATION

Configuration data for each machine should be tracked in detail on forms similar to this one. This format is quite crowded and should be expanded onto a second page to provide sufficient space to document information about peripheral devices. Additional information about compatibility may need to be noted in a narrative field.

EQUIPMENT MAINTENANCE RECORD

An Equipment Maintenance Record is used to keep a continuous record of actions taken to repair equipment. Future troubleshooting is aided by knowing whether previous problems have occurred. Ideally, this form could be used to also note upgrades and software installations so that the time sequence of events is maintained.

Both forms may be downloaded from this book's Website, *www.smu. edu/~nhowden/micros.html*.

MICROCOMPUTER CONFIGURATION

INVENTORY DATA

Our serial number:		Assigned to:	
Location:		Phone number:	
E-mail address:			

MANUFACTURER DATA

Item & Model Number:
Manufacturer:
Warranty Period:
Manufacturer's Serial Number:

PO#		PO DATE: / /	RECEIVED: / /

Vendor Name:
Vendor Phone:
Vendor Address:

CONFIGURATION DATA

DRIVE INFORMATION			CPU INFORMATION		CARD INFORMATION	
	Type	Size	CPU Type:		Slot 1:	
A:			Speed:		Slot 2:	
B:			RAM:		Slot 3:	
C:			Other Features		Slot 4:	
D:			Watts?		Slot 5:	
CD-ROM:			Serial Port?		Slot 6:	
Tape Drive:			Parallel Port?		Slot 7:	
Type of Monitor:					Slot 8:	

PERIPHERAL DEVICES				
Item name	Model Number	Notes	Quantity	Inventory Number

EQUIPMENT MAINTENANCE RECORD

Item & Model Number:		
Inventory Number:		*Manufacturer's Serial Number:*
Maintenance Vendor Name:		
Phone Number:	*FAX Number:*	
Address:		
Period of coverage:		
PO Number:	*PO Date:*	
Problem:	*Date called in:*	*Spoke to:*
Notes:		
Problem:	*Date called in:*	*Spoke to:*
Notes:		
Problem:	*Date called in:*	*Spoke to:*
Notes:		
Problem:	*Date called in:*	*Spoke to:*
Notes:		
Problem:	*Date called in:*	*Spoke to:*
Notes:		
Problem:	*Date called in:*	*Spoke to:*
Notes:		

APPENDIX H: CONFIGURATION MANAGEMENT

Configuration information for all machines needs to be related together for particular kinds of troubleshooting and management decision making. Network configuration or setup of database services often requires knowing IP numbers and adapter addresses. Establishing maintenance contracts may require knowing how many machines are still under warranty.

This form may be downloaded from this book's Website, *www.smu. edu/~nhowden/micros.html*.

CONFIGURATION MANAGEMENT

	Machine #	Machine #	Machine #	Machine #
Make				
Model				
Serial Number				
Inventory Number				
Date of Purchase				
PO Number				
CPU speed				
HD type & size				
Memory				
Monitor Size				
Network Interface?				
IP Address				
Physical Location				
Type of Utilization				

APPENDIX I: COMPUTER MAINTENANCE TOOLS

BASIC COLLECTION

Screwdrivers
    flat head (2 sizes)
    Phillips head (2 sizes)
Small flashlight
Socket drivers
Torque drivers
Mosquito-nosed (curved) hemostat
Spare screws & jumper
Small hand vacuum or compressed air
Small pocketknife
Toolbox
Wireless telephone with line jack in library public area (may require
    an analog phone line)

BENCH STOCK

Spare cables (IDE, power, "Y" adapter, SVGA)
PS/2 to DIN 5 keyboard adapter
Serial to PS/2 mouse adapter
Keyboard extension cable
Network cable ends
Spare miniature nuts & bolts
Floppy disks and Zip disks

NETWORK CABLING

Bulk cable (CAT5 twisted pair or RG59 coax)
Cable ends (RJ45 or BNC)
75 Ohm terminating resistors (for coax)
Crimpers (RJ11 and RJ45 or coax)
Wire cutters
"Drop cables" in precut lengths

OPTIONAL

Digital multimeter
Television/monitor alignment tools
Keyboard key puller
Macintosh case cracker
LAN Analyzer
Oscilloscope
Wire strippers

INDEX

ABOUT THE AUTHOR

Norman Howden has served as an academic information specialist, developed and managed an information center at Louisiana State University, and taught in Schools of Library and Information Science at LSU, the University of North Texas, and the University of Missouri. In each of those schools his teaching introduced students to facets of library technology. Throughout his career, Dr. Howden has managed computer labs, installed and operated local area networks, and managed many types of software including both networked and desktop software. Over the past two decades he has budgeted for, purchased, and installed innumerable types of software.

Dr. Howden began life as a military brat, which affected his educational experiences from the beginning. He attended four different high schools in Paris, Texas; Taipei; Tokyo, and Yorktown, Virginia. He went on to work on a B.S. at Central Missouri State University. After an eight year stint in the military he went back to school to earn an M.A.L.S. from the University of Missouri. From there he completed a Ph.D. at Case Western Reserve University in Cleveland.

Dr. Howden is currently an Assistant Dean of Learning Resources at El Centro College and also serves as an Information Specialist at the Business Information Center in the Cox School of Business at Southern Methodist University, both in Dallas. Dr. Howden has conducted and funded projects and authored a number of journal articles, books, and thesauruses in library and information science. Over the last two years his professional work has included developing electronic course reserves for El Centro College, implementing pay-for-print systems, purchasing new computers and other technology, developing introductory Web courses, and conducting bibliographic instruction. His areas of current interest include management of technology resources, indexing development, and use of business resources.